ISBN: 0-578-50247-X
ISBN-13: 978-0-578-50247-2

Dedication to My Mother

Mom, this book is dedicated to you. Thank you for raising me to be the strong woman I am today, the one you always saw me to be.

That strength taught me to break free & finally do what you wanted to all of your life but never could, speak up. Thank you for allowing me the courage to break my personal Omertà once & for all and to help women and children living in fear. Thank you for the gift of bravery.

All the times you said to me, "Maria, one day you'll be able to leave here, fly high & reach beyond the stars." I truly believe the song "Wind Beneath My Wings" was written just for the two of us.

Love Your Daughter,

Maria

This book is dedicated to all the people living in darkness who are suffering in silence behind invisible prison walls that seem unimaginable to break free from …

For all of us who are used to wearing masks for others to see but are dying on the inside …

For the women and children living at the hands of domestic violence as a reminder that change is possible; not only possible but a real option …

The choice is yours even if you have been told differently and know that help is always here for you …

No matter what you are going through, don't let fear hold you back. Use it to propel you forward. My goal is that you let the lessons I share in this book become the key for you to break free…

Based on the true inspirational story of Maria
co-written with Sheila Brody

INTRODUCTION

If you are reading this book because you want to get an insight into deep mob secrets or find out who whacked who or who did what to whom in the mob world, you should close this book right now. The real gangsters, mobsters and Italian Mafia are not the focus here.

The word mobster can take on many different descriptions. When you look up the word mobster in the dictionary - okay, scratch that - when you Google the word mobster, the definition is simple, *"A member of a group of violent criminals; a gangster, a person of violence"* In my home, the word mobster was synonymous with monster.

This book comes from a deep desire to share my story of transformation. For each person living in pain of any kind, there is someone who transformed their pain to show you it is possible to change any life circumstance. My transformation brought me from growing up at the hands of a monster to breaking free from that abuse and creating my own life.

My intent is to share my story so that other people can see what is possible in their world and say, "If she can do it, so can I. I can get through this and become better, no matter the circumstances that surround me".

Achievements, changes and transformations cut through circumstances of all descriptions without exception. When the words are backed by action and all the excuses are removed, great things happen.

This is my story, compiled from decades of journal and diary entries. It is written from my point of view and reveals the energies behind what shaped me as a person and the journey that turned me upside down and inside out to get to the core of my truth.

It's all here, my Italian, mobster, gangsta, Howard Beach, non-ratting family story.

So here we go ...

A Few Things First

I learned many lessons growing up in my neighborhood that stuck with me throughout my life. Strength. Loyalty. Integrity. Family. And the Rules of the Game.

Strength.

It is amazing how much a person can take before breaking. That's the challenge in the mob life; people crack or break under pressure. They "rat" or they make up stories about someone else rather than stand in their own strength. From weakness can only be found more weakness. Early on as a child, I decided to be strong and not allow myself to crumble to my circumstances or to anyone else's agenda. I would control one thing for sure, who I was going to be!

Loyalty.

If you look up the word loyalty you'll find something like, *"The quality of being loyal to someone or something"* or *"a strong feeling of support or allegiance"*.

Growing up, I heard people say, "she was loyal to her husband all those years" or in my neighborhood, "she showed her loyalty to her husband while he was away all those years".

United we stand. Our support and our allegiances were to our family. And our family reached well beyond the four walls in our home. Family was, and is, a strong word to be shared with the people you spend your time with. The people who treat you with respect. The people who are loyal and truthful with their word and who have your back. Always. In all ways.

When we say, "I got your back", we pledge not to ever drive a knife into it. We care for our family. When we break bread with each other, it is like an oath we take to care for and protect one another. Trust is everything.

Integrity.

Your integrity tells a story about who you really are and where you come from. Not geographically on a map, but who you really are. Who you are shines through your eyes from your heart and soul. Integrity shapes the intentions behind all the decisions you choose to make. It communicates who you are to the universe louder than any of my Italian family dinners; without making a sound.

Family.

Where I come from you just don't rat on your family or your friends. Hell, you don't even rat on people you're not that close with. I think the old saying blood is thicker than water came from my neck of the woods in Howard Beach. Whether or not we were related by blood, we created our own thickness and viscosity based on our word. So our family, we would choose.

You were initiated into a group of like-minded individuals who knew everything about you and you knew everything about them.

Why is this important?

Because your family is everything, it is all you will ever have. Our family becomes our blood connection. I always admired and respected the fact we could choose and love our family. It is a gift not to be taken lightly.

Rules of the Game.

There are some rules to be a mobster, gangster or a boss of any kind, really. You stay true to yourself and don't go against the family code. Family code can be changed to work, business, team, etc. I got the picture very early on to keep my word and my honor with anyone I chose to become close with. My word and my honor were all I had and everything I knew.

So, my word, I would keep. My mouth, I would shut about other people's business.

I know the rules. I follow the rules. There is no going against the rules for me. In order to respect the rules, I first had to learn them.

I learned the rules for a "sit down". A sit down is a negotiation, a chance to understand the other person and come to a mutually acceptable outcome. Notice, I did not say everyone likes the outcome; just that everyone understands and agrees to the outcome.

The rules of a sit down are simple:

1.   You must come willing to communicate and always tell your truth. About any situation. No matter what.

2.   There must be two or more people present along with supporting characters that may be needed. But only the important decision makers may agree on the terms.

3.   You must come with respect for all parties. You are encouraged to stick up for yourself and stay strong but being disrespectful to each other is

frowned upon. Since it can be and usually is an ego game, it doesn't hurt to be cordial and not beat your chest too much. *Unfortunately, this rule is very rarely followed.*

If no agreement is reached between the parties, the "Boss" makes the decision about what happens next.

There's one thing you can't bring to a sit down. You cannot bring fear! People don't respect fear. If fear enters your aura, then you are screwed.

If you think about it a sit down is kinda like life. You can either be angry and try to argue with life or you can agree to work with life.

Life will give you anything you ask for as long as you play by its rules. The same rules apply. Speak your truth. Respect others. And do not live in fear.

CAST OF CHARACTERS

THE DOMESTICATOR

Let's talk about the word domestication. We are all domesticated by our parents/guardians, no different from a dog. A dog responds to a series of rewards for acceptable behavior with a treat and learns unacceptable behaviors with a punishment. I liken my upbringing to that of a dog; being controlled to be what the domesticator thought I should be.

My domesticator was my father.

Mom had enormous pressure to have boys. He told her that girls are useless and that he hates women, so she was ordered to push out the boys. My mother gave him a son and then came me.

I was born in the spring of 1970. When the doctor proclaimed, "It's a girl!", the domesticator shrugged and said, "it should have been a boy".

But I wasn't a boy. I was a beautiful, eight-pound, healthy little girl that would turn out to be one hundred times the man he would ever be.

"King of the Castle"… that was his description of himself. He ruled his Kingdom with fear, anger and threats. Real threats. Not like today's kind of threats of "finish your carrots or no iPad", or "you have to take a time out." There was no hesitation. It was all action.

If you did something that he didn't like, you got a beating; right then and there. Verbal or physical, his choice, of course. No apologies and no regrets.

"If you cry, I'll give you a reason to cry." *Crack!* Right across the face. Or the head. Or the back.

His belt was his best friend. Not to keep his pants up, but to keep his family in check. I remember hearing the cries and screams from each of my brothers and they would cry out for Mom and she would come in and, of course, catch her beating too. We eventually stopped calling for her because there was no reason all of us had to "get it".

The most frustrating thing became hearing others "catching it." Especially Mom. There is something so unbelievably crushing for a young girl to hear her mother pleading for her life while her father threatened to kill her in front of his children.

Was it true? Would he kill her right there in front of me? Please God, I'll be good. I'll do better. I'll be a good girl. Please make him stop hurting Mommy.

It was easier to feel the physical pain, rather than the anguish of hearing others cry out for help and not be able to do anything. It was better to be beaten than to helplessly stand by.

These are the moments I learned how to tune out and cut off from abuse in my life.

My grandparents could only listen from upstairs, living right above us, they had many sleepless nights praying for the cries to stop.

"What are you doing?" Grandpa's strong voice would ask.

"Go upstairs. Mind your business!" The Domesticator would scream. They knew if they got involved, it wouldn't matter, and he would take it out on us even more. They would have no choice but to retreat to their apartment upstairs. After the beatings I would go to them to be held and consoled. It was the only place where I would feel love within the building that we called "home".

He had consequences for everything. Every single thing was assessed through his magnifying glass. He wouldn't miss a thing. Each consequence would be implemented immediately.

"I'll show you not to do that again." *Crack.*

"How dare you!" *Crack.*

His blows were not just disciplinary either. The domesticator would lose it over anything. If he was having a bad day, and we were in the way? *Crack.* Didn't finish dinner? *Crack.* Mom did something that he didn't like? You guessed it. *Crack.*

I remember getting caught smoking a cigarette and he turned to the devil. I knew lies like "I was holding it for a friend" or "it wasn't mine" wouldn't work. There was no lying. Lying made it ten times worse. The one thing he despised more than women, were liars, and he was paranoid about us lying. Or turning into a liar. It was amazing that in his quest for people not lying, he molded and created liars.

My mother turned into the biggest liar I ever knew. She lied to protect all of us. She was our shield and sacrificed herself so we could survive.

I used to ask what came first? The lies or the

beatings and then more lies not to get beaten again.

All the beatings, lying and living in fear left my mom paranoid and distrustful. Her communication about the hurt she endured at his hands is non-existent. She has no outlet except for my aunt who is her very best friend and confidant.

My mom never broke her own personal Omertà. This woman could be hung upside down by her toenails and not say a thing.

Growing up, it was my job to clean, clean and then clean again. I would have to get up early and clean the entire house. I would do the laundry, wash the dishes and make the beds so tight that you could bounce a quarter off the sheets. I kid you not, if it didn't bounce off the tightly fitted sheets, tucked in each corner with the pillows placed perfectly (the open sides toward the middle) then the bed wasn't made.

It had to be perfect every time and there was

not an hour or a day that would go by that the beds were left unmade.

As children, we had to tiptoe in and out of his "kingdom" as not to disturb him.

Not just the kids, his wife too.

It was always quiet in His Kingdom unless he decided it would be okay for that moment or for his favorite son or however he decided to move the chess pieces around the board on that particular day. I knew we were all playing his game together.

I am a team player to my core but didn't have a team environment in my home. We were broken and I was benched most of the time.

I often asked myself, why this game? Why was he playing so one sided, did he like having an unfair advantage over children? Who made up the rules to this game anyway? There was no map, cheat sheet or directions on our box.

I couldn't see the bigger picture. Nothing was clear about the game the domesticator played except that it created a family filled with FEAR. We had to play along as prompted by his moves. I had to do as I was told or face the consequences.

On weekends, when I ran out of things to clean in the house, he would lead me into the garage or the backyard to make sure everything was in tip top shape.

When we shoveled the snow in the New York winters, he would sit at the window and peer out to see how the path was coming along.

Tap tap tap. His finger would point to a spot that was missed, and then he would sink back into his comfy chair and continue reading his paper. We would take a break but as soon as the shovel stopped scraping across the concrete …

Tap. Tap. Tap.

"No cutting corners. Let's go, get it done, we have more to get done today". I learned to check things off my list, relentlessly and bring projects to the finish line every time without cutting corners.

I was kept on task in order to keep me in check and keep me away from trouble. Trouble was whatever outside element he decided was bad - like boys. He wanted me nowhere near boys.

I was allowed to hang out only with the Nuns in high school, but never allowed to go away to a convent retreat with them. He said no every chance he got. I asked Sister Jane to ask him for me. She told him that she would personally watch over me, no boys would be there and I could stay with her. She told him that the entire class was going and that it was a Holy trip where I would learn to be closer to God.

He still said no. The entire class went. The entire girl's school with the Nuns.

Everyone except me. There were things to do.

Now when the domesticator was out at the club, things were great. He hung out at the social club in my neighborhood. It was where the men would go to discuss business, have a drink, smoke cigars and play cards.

When he grabbed the car keys, we would all breathe a sigh of relief. A little peace and relaxation. But not for too long, because he would always swing the door back open and make his demands.

Day after day; the same old thing.

When his friends came to meet at our house and discuss more important business, it was everybody out. We weren't even allowed to stay in our own house. It didn't even matter what time of day or evening they would come. I would sit and wonder what they were talking about. What was so important that his entire family had to wait outside? Even his elderly mother and his wife! It never seemed normal to me.

But normal or sane, he was not, so I just dealt with it, without question.

Time and time again.

I would be glad when the men would come

over to talk. It meant I didn't have to be involved with him that night. I would go to my friend's house and they would take care of me.

My neighbors' and friends' houses were the places where I would learn how a normal family behaved. I would share smiles and laughter and see how a real man who earned the title "Dad" could be so loving to his wife and children.

It felt so nice to see and feel the love. This was where I realized exactly what I wanted in this lifetime and I would do everything to get.

I saw love as an outsider and never really felt it in my home, so I created it in my mind. There was no "I love you" or compassionate conversation from the domesticator. I don't know if he knew how to speak those type of words. Those words and feelings seemed to be his kryptonite.

I would create my own love and my own family one day.

GRANDMA

To find out why The Domesticator was the way he was, I started to dig deeper into his upbringing.

Grandma was beautiful and she attracted very good men that would love and care for her and her family. Her first husband, the domesticator's father, died in the war and she married the only Grandpa I knew. When someone would comment on my amazing grandpa, the domesticator would fiercely say, "That's not their real grandfather." He had true hatred for such a wonderful person that was a mentor to him and to me and my brothers. The domesticator hated him and his own mother for bringing a father figure into their home.

After her first husband died, my grandmother was left to raise her two young boys alone. I believe the domesticator always wanted to be the man of the house and take care of her and his brother. He was way too young and Grandma knew this, so she did what every amazing single mom does today, but was so rare back then, she got a job.

A single mom in the 1950s went off to work.

She worked at Macmillan Publishers and although her title was 'Secretary', she was functioning as the company's Financial Controller. Since women couldn't hold such positions or titles at that time, Secretary was her title and dictated her salary.

It was an amazing time in New York City, as she would tell me. She had a lifelong friend and co-worker, named Mary Patterson, who was a dark-skinned, African American woman.

Grandma loved Mary. On lunch breaks they would walk together, arm and arm, down Fifth Avenue and ignore ugly comments about their friendship from uneducated racists. People on the street would comment and say mean things, but the pair kept on trucking. Grandma worked for

Macmillan for forty years and only retired when she got the guts to ask for a raise and the company responded to her with a firm no. So she left.

There's nothing more gangsta than a woman with a mind of her own.

She would survive two husbands and a companion with whom she fell in love with in her 80s. She cared for him until his passing. They didn't marry, but she was every part of a wife to that man. My grandmother, the domesticator's mother, passed away in 2013.

My mother and I were her caretakers until the end. We walked her through her last steps in life and she drew her last breath in my arms. It was a beautiful moment. One I will never forget. It is quite difficult to explain the beauty and the bond this experience lends to the person passing and the one helping them cross over.

I coached Grandma through her last breath

peacefully and with love. All the love in the world was in her room at that hour and the bond was so beautiful and everlasting. I saw her dancing in the beautiful light above and she encourages me to this day to keep breaking free, every chance I get.

The one person missing was the domesticator. The one man she wanted to love her but from whom she would never get love. I still can't piece together why she wanted him there with her after all those years of him ignoring her. All the time that went by where he didn't care about her and on her deathbed, all she could do was ask for him.

I guess a mother's love for her child crosses all barriers.

GRANDPA #1

Still digging deep, I wanted to look into each player's role. Grandma's first husband, whom she loved dearly, was off fighting for our country when he passed away.

It wasn't in a hail of bullets, it was an aneurysm in his chest, but tragic all the same. Grandpa was sent home from the war extremely ill and lost his life at an early age.

I came across a letter my great-uncle wrote in 1947 so my uncle and the domesticator could know who their father was. It lives today as an organic artifact from the past that captures a moment of what was happening during those years. A relic I had the opportunity to read, study and learn from. I believe it was written just for me. It might as well have read, *"Dear Maria,"*.

The letter also shed light on a rare congenital blood disorder called HHT, also known as Osler-Weber-Rendu disease. HHT is an inherited disorder that causes abnormal connections to develop between arteries and veins. It can affect multiple organs of the body. HHT is still often misdiagnosed and many doctors do not understand all of its manifestations.

After my grandfather returned from the war, he was brought to Staten Island Hospital and then sent to Washington DC for months of testing to help him with his dangerous situation. He was the first to undergo aneurysm surgery in the country and possibly the world.

After reading the letter from my great-uncle and talking to my family, it seemed there was a lot of love back then for the domesticator, my uncle and the rest of our family. What went so wrong that twisted the domesticator's mind so much that he thought it was okay to mentally, emotionally and physically abuse his family?

MY MOTHER

My mother would tell me that we were lucky because we would be able to grow up and move out. She would say, "When you're a little older, you can go then." I remember saying, "You mean we. We can go then, right Ma?"

"Umm yes. Of course we, Maria. We can go then," she would say or "It's not time, now. When your baby brother gets a little bigger, then the time will be right." or "When you're in high school Maria, then we will go."

I can remember her packing small things inside Tupperware and pretending it was food for a friend. *Did she think he would ask her to open the lasagna dish to check it?* Stuff kept leaving the house, into her trunk and unpacked in her mother's basement in Valley Stream. She would move our stuff little by little.

"When we get all of our things there, then we will leave," she would proclaim. That was the plan and I was okay with it, because we had this plan. So, little by little it was.

Soon she graduated to boxes, duffle bags and then finally a suitcase! I would think my prayers were answered when the suitcase was packed up with clothes and items from around the house. It was finally my time to be in an environment ruled by love! Grandma Rose's house had enough love for all of us.

This packing and unpacking, I would soon find out, was a lie. It was all to appease me. Soon all the boxes, bags and Tupperware came back into our house. How could this be? She wasn't going anywhere. Years would pass, then decades. She always knew she would not escape.

The last time I asked was before my 16th birthday.

"After your Sweet 16. Everyone is coming to it, Maria. How could we go now?"

What else was I supposed to do but believe her? She was my mom and teaching me how to "deal with it".

Her way to "deal with it" was to fall subservient to his demands. My skin would crawl when I would witness the way he would speak to her and the look was worse than his words. His eyes told a story to her that only they shared. A story that he would hold over her head for their entire life. I would never know what it was, but I knew the end of the story was "or I'll kill ya".

I knew she deserved more, we all did. I knew there was a freedom out there, peace and eventually love. Definitely love.

We could learn to love and support each other much better in a healthier environment where mom wouldn't be with someone she despised, and my baby bro wouldn't have to shake with fear while watching his mom get humiliated. A place where mom could make up her own mind as to what she wanted to do each day and she would learn to say more and share her feelings.

One day I prayed for her to open her mouth and all her love and feelings would come rushing out for me. I pictured her being able to talk about the violence and our family being able to heal through it together. Then I remembered his threats and that she was filled with fear.

All the "shut your mouths, keep quiets and I'll kill ya's" she heard throughout her lifetime added up. I knew she would never be able to speak up. *We don't talk about anything. It's a rule.* Our conversations were all fake. They were shallow, shadowed by fear, and just surface talk to get through to the next moment.

MY BABY BRO

My baby brother was Mamma's baby boy. He and mom have always had a special bond. She would, as she did with all of us, pray that the beatings would stop in time for him to be saved from the torture. She would think that since he was the baby, several years younger than the rest of us, perhaps the domesticator would start to slow down. She would try to keep him hidden from the torture, but there was no hiding in HIS house.

Not for his wife, his children, the baby or even the dog. NO ONE would escape in the domesticator's kingdom.

My little brother didn't get as many physical beatings as the rest of us but was equally tortured mentally as he was forced to watch. He would have to sit and watch everything through a set of iron bars behind the living room staircase. His little body trembling and tears running down his cheeks as he watched what was happening to his mom.

He was too young to be able to do anything. Too young, but tortured just the same.

My baby brother was 15 when the domesticator kicked him out on the street. I remember thinking, *he's gotta get his own apartment? And work at 15? There's no way Mom will let that happen. There besties and he is her baby boy. There is just no way.*

I started thinking about how this would play out. *Oh, this was it! Now was our time.*

We would all be able to stay together. I figured mom would never allow her baby to live on his own without parents at 15. He wasn't allowed back in the house, so we would finally get to move out together and leave the domesticator for good! I put a bag aside and helped sneak a few of his things out to him. I wanted to pack his records because he was a DJ and it would really hurt to leave those behind, but I knew I couldn't do that because I knew the consequences there would be in the house.

My baby brother got a job working at The Limelight as one of the supporting DJs.

He would pick me and my friends up and then pick up "Desire," a gorgeous six and a half foot tall drag queen and off we would go. I always admired that my bro was so comfortable around so many different types of people without judgement.

The Limelight was the top club in New York City in the 90s. One that catered to the emerging enormous New York City drug scene. Tripping on ecstasy and crack cocaine were newly spoken around my age group; along with the holdovers from the 70s and 80s - cocaine, acid and pills.

The place was alive. The music and the scene were outrageous. The place was huge. You could get lost in the maze of different rooms with all kinds of music. Rave. Rap and Reggae. House music.

There were private rooms with erotic dancing and drug dens. There were scaffolding type stairs and overhangs to see the enormous crowd on the main dance floor. Couches lined the back walls and made for quiet areas for people in "k" holes, to regroup and sober up.

As you can imagine, working at The Limelight and living on your own was no way for a 15 year old to be spending his time. The fear of what could happen to him out there all alone absolutely crushed me. I couldn't believe he wouldn't be able to live with us any longer.

I had no choice but to deal with it, all the good and the bad that would come out of him growing up inside The Limelight. No words.

THE BOSS

The Domesticator proudly called my middle brother, "The Boss".

He would be the Boss of the bathroom. *Yes, that was a real thing.* The Boss of the house. The Boss of … whatever. A seed was planted early on that he would be a Boss, or in charge in his lifetime.

We always got along well, The Boss and me. We would play stoop ball, swim in our family pool, pitch quarters on the corner and play Skully at Charles Park.

He was a good kid and I always knew he would become an entrepreneur. He worked hard from the moment anyone let him. We started a paper route together as kids. When he was 11 or 12, he started at our local deli and then got a job at the auto parts yard. He would work and work and work until he was called the Boss. Later, he would actually be the boss of his own successful company.

When we were all young, a family member brought us Christmas gifts. Cabbage Patch dolls.

My middle brother and I were close in age and Cabbage Patch dolls were all the rage. They were the "must have" gift that year. Everyone wanted one.

My doll's name was Darcy Rhoda and had brown hair and brown eyes. My brother got a boy Cabbage Patch doll with short brown hair and brown eyes. Our eyes lit up when we saw them because they were sold out at every toy store and impossible to come by. And there they were right in front of us. We were absolutely delighted! For about a minute.

When the domesticator saw my brother with the doll, he absolutely lost it.

"My boy is not gonna play with a doll! Never going to happen." He ripped the doll out of his son's hands before he even got to fully take it out of the box. He ripped the doll's head off and tore the doll to pieces. The doll was left in pieces on the floor for us to see. No one would dare clean it up. It was our lesson to look at it.

He turned on Mom, "Let another doll enter this house and see what happens. No son of mine will ever play with a doll." He blamed Mom, as usual. Everything was her fault and she caught one for that, I am certain.

It wasn't long before everyone in our circle knew never to bring dolls to our house. And I never saw another doll enter my house after that day.

"Killing" my brother's doll was not enough for the domesticator. He still had the need to break on my brother and tease him relentlessly about it.

"Do you miss your doll? Huh, do you? Do you care about that thing? Speak up, I can't hear you. You want to play with dolls, huh, speak up boy."

"You better not want to play with dolls. Do you like to play with dolls like a girl?"

It was a trick question. Even if my brother

wanted to play with the doll more than anything, he learned very young that he could never say that. Just take his boy approved truck, suck it up and move on. He was only a kid but learned very quickly that DOLLS were OUT.

Being a BOSS was IN.

NEEDLENOSE

My oldest brother was nicknamed Needlenose. In fairness, we all had big Italian noses in our house, but he was very tall for a kid, and I guess his nose was appropriately larger to fit his frame. He was the class clown in school and in our family. I looked up to him and was his tag along little sister.

Humor was a huge part of life at our house. It got our family through so much fear and sadness. Needlenose made us laugh and laugh and forget the terror of the domesticator for a while. I thought he was funny even when he used to fart, roll the windows up in the car and then lock them. He was always distracting me from the pain I felt inside and I will love and cherish him for that forever.

I believe Needlenose's domestication had him cut off from his family. It's sad to cut people off who love you. He learned that from the domesticator so I don't blame him for his behavior toward me.

The blame, not the excuse. Each of us get to choose our path, no matter our life circumstances, upbringing or any myriad of excuses that we could use to justify our actions. I don't offer excuses, so I don't accept any. To me, family is family. I never understood throwing your family away for no good reason, especially when you go through such a challenging upbringing and make it through together.

I do know that I was taught never to talk about anything. Perhaps that was it. A learned behavior that could be unlearned, I hope.

Family is everything to me.

MY VERY FIRST ANGEL

I believe that there are certain people in our lives that are there to provide love and guidance. They become our living angels.

Every year I was allowed to go on a trip to Florida by myself and stay with my Aunt Eva and my cousins.

Unlike the domesticator who didn't want a girl and threw me into a door when I was six years old because he was angry my mother cut my hair short, Aunt Eva treated me like a princess. She always allowed me to dress in pretty clothes, brushed my hair and kissed me goodnight on my forehead after tucking me in bed.

I felt loved, safe and special when I was with her. Eva was more than my aunt, she was my angel and she helped me plant seeds of love deep within me that I would later fight to harvest.

GROWING UP

Blood makes you related, loyalty makes you family.

I grew up in Howard Beach, New York. It's a small neighborhood on the border of Brooklyn and Queens, separating the Broad Channel in the Rockaways with East New York in Brooklyn.

Growing up on the beach, I learned a few more rules to live by: don't ask questions, keep your mouth shut about anything you see, and you don't rat on nobody for no reason.

Families were shamed if anyone ever thought they betrayed or sold out someone from our town to save themselves. It's one reason I think parts of

Florida got so popular over the years.

It is simply a matter of respect. Respect is everything.

Howard Beach also borders JFK International Airport. I think of the many conversations that happened when the planes flew low over Charles Park. They flew so low over the park that it seemed they were coming through the windows of our homes. The entire house would shake, and you had to scream loud if you wanted anyone to hear you. Because of this, it set the perfect backdrop for a meeting to whisper in someone's ear *if you didn't want anyone to hear what you were saying.*

The passionate talk and whispers will only be known by the few who sat on the benches overlooking the water at the crest of the park. The important conversations would conveniently be timed with the landing of the Concord, which would roar in the mornings and afternoons in the late 90s.

Just like the Concord protected conversation from being overheard, I decided to build a wall to protect myself from hearing all the noise in my own head. My emotional roller coaster would bring me up and then eventually down to feelings of despair. False promises would carry me to euphoric heights and then the bottom would drop out as the roller coaster plummeted and I would close my eyes and hold on until it was over.

It seemed pretty simple to me. No feelings = no let downs = no hurt. Not sharing emotions was "aOK" with me. I actually preferred it.

Emotions felt noisy. I couldn't figure them out. They just got in the way. I couldn't cry and I couldn't laugh so I built a wall. I locked my feelings up in an old chest and buried it behind that wall. Brick by brick, I built the wall that would create the space between freedom and fear. I was the mason, the architect and the bricks themselves. The wall I built was tall and wide enough to keep the hurt away from me, well most of it anyhow.

I realized I was alone in this world and I would protect myself at all costs. So I stayed behind my wall where no one could hurt me.

People would feel bad or sorry for me after learning of the abuse. They would give me their pity and say, "No one should ever go through that, especially a young girl".

I saw it as just his way. This may sound a bit harsh to some people. The way I survived was to cut off from my emotions. The fear of knowing the next beating was just around the corner was one I didn't need. Yes, there were six of us in the house, but I felt alone.

There were rewards for being the person he wanted you to be. Those rewards came in the package of money, diamonds, jewelry, cars, ect.

And there were punishments. Beatings were

pretty standard in my house; mental, emotional, psychological, and physical, we had them all. It was dispensed regularly without rhyme or reason by this out of control bipolar person; we could all count on our daily dose.

"Go to your room, and don't come out until you know why I sent you there," the domesticator would shout and I would hear the door lock behind me.

Children. Wife. Dog. It really didn't matter. Everyone would learn his or her lesson.

And yes, I said dog.

I think about what that defenseless dog did to deserve being abused. I imagine what might have been going through that dog's mind when the person he served and loved was mistreating him. I know he felt helpless, that poor dog. I know because I too was helpless to the master I was serving.

The domesticator locked my mother out on the porch one night, in the cold with no shoes and no jacket. It was her punishment for something she did, or something we did and her covering it up for us. It seemed to me that he wanted us kids to learn a lesson by hearing her cries and feeling the fear of her freezing. Nothing mattered but his viewpoint and creating fear so that we would all obey him.

God forbid one of the kids wanted to unlock the door. If we tried to help her, we were warned very sternly not to go near the door. Pleading and begging for him to let her in was worse. How embarrassing is that for a grown woman to go through?

I wanted to help her. I had always been a solutionizer™. *Yes, that is a word*. I thought about planning to outsmart him next time. All I could think about is how we could preplan to ensure she would be safe. I thought about putting a key under the doormat so next time she could get in. I wanted to tell her my idea the next night but quickly remembered that even though the key would be there, she couldn't ever use it to open the door. Or we would both get it even more.

So shaky and quiet we stayed. We were trained to stay quiet. No tears. We were told to think about why she was locked out.

Then his dreaded voice yells for me, "Maria!" I have no choice but to answer.

"Come here!"

Squeamishly, I shuffled over to him to see what was going to happen.

"Refill my glass of soda with ice."

Our teachers knew. The Nuns knew. The Priest knew. The Principal knew. But no one dared get involved. You see, they were all part of their own Omertà. That secret code of silence; of "keeping it shut."

We didn't talk about the abuse. I would look to the adults I had in my life for guidance but we both knew that I just had to do what I had to do to endure this upbringing. I couldn't say anything.

"Maria, what happened to your eye?"

"Oh nothing Sister, I fell. Can I go now?" I hated lying the most, but I knew I had to. I couldn't say he sent me to school with my eye busted because I lied to him about something.

Every house on the block was always open for us and Mom. We were treated as if we were part of their family. They gave us safety, peace, serenity and most importantly to me - love.

But no one could tell me why this was happening or why the domesticator couldn't control himself.

Did some people have sit downs with him? Of course. My neighbor's dad had sit downs with him. My mom's brother and my uncles all sat down with the guy, but I think he couldn't help himself.

It was who he was. It was in his DNA.

Adolescence, as you might imagine, was awkward for a young woman growing up in this environment. I was going through physical, mental, emotional and spiritual changes. I was becoming a woman in his kingdom.

I was a tough girl, never backing down from a fight and fiercely sticking up for my friends and family. Inside, I was just waiting for someone to mess with me or my people. I was looking to take out my anger on others.

I was so angry and filled with fear, I did not want to deal with this life anymore. I really didn't want to die but I didn't know how to live. I wanted to feel physical pain to numb the mental pain and violence I was going through. I was sad and depressed, constantly reliving each day in my house. I was caught in a place of reliving the past and developing anxiety about the future. I was living in fear.

The cries of "please don't" or "please stop" became a habit and a way to react.

When I was around 15 years old, I decided to seek out my own escape from the pain. I had to stop the thinking, the voices and all the noise in my head. It had to stop.

A crack is all I needed to release the pain. I couldn't find one and so I decided to create one in my body. I did what I was taught over and over. Inflict pain and learn a lesson.

I wanted to learn how to get the hell out of the fearful place so I would violently inflict pain on myself. I would punch my chest until I bruised, hit my head on things to unleash the feelings. I would cut my flesh and the hurt, anguish and pain would have a path to escape.

"Go to your room and think about what you did and don't come out until you know why I sent you in there," he would say. Locked in my room, it was just me.

I would just sit in my room and think about the shame, guilt, fear and anger over and over again.

I needed to escape but couldn't get out. The noise got so loud that I tried to slice my wrist with a knife. I heard if you cut your wrist that you could escape everything.

Thankfully, the blade wasn't sharp. Truthfully, it was probably about as sharp as a butter knife and didn't do much damage. I really didn't want to die. I just needed to dull the pain and cut it out of my body.

I never told anyone, I just kept it shut, like I was taught to do. I was told not to talk about anything to anyone for any reason.

Thinking back to that time, I am truly grateful for the outlets I did have. Without them I wouldn't have made it through. I would have kept reaching for a sharper tool until I eventually found one.

My Sweet 16 was just around the corner. I would have been happy with a boombox in the back yard dancing all night to Whitney, Michael, and Madonna, but my family had to go all out.

I still remember that custom made royal blue dress. I looked like a Spanish Quinceanera in spaghetti straps, fierce gazelles and my corsage. Puffy hair completed the look.

My party was an event. Everyone was there. A couple of hundred people packed into La Bella Vita in Ozone Park.

A three-tiered chocolate cake with butter creme frosting and a large cake topper sat on a dais in front of the dance floor. Uniformed service stood behind a buffet of twenty different kinds of food, ready to serve. Champagne bottles dotted every table.

My Sweet 16 gift was a diamond necklace. It was from him, but it was nice and I was grateful for it. I was not impressed by his "show prize," but I was happy to have something of my own. I daydreamed that this necklace fell off a truck, so I wouldn't have the emotion of being thankful to him or ever have to owe him anything. Falling off a truck or not, it was the first thing I had of my very own.

Strangely, I never saw any of the gift envelopes that were handed to him from my family, friends, uncles, neighbors, local guys at the club or anyone else.

I thought that was pretty cool since I didn't want to accept anything from him, so this was perfect. I actually paid for my necklace and my party.

I wanted to owe nothing so I'd never hear him say the words, "you owe me" or "after what I have done for you". *Nope, nothing like that would ever even enter his mind.*

It's all good. I won't ever owe him a thing in my life. I got my necklace, which I paid for with my unopened gifts and dreamed about my freedom.

"Just be happy he got you that beautiful diamond necklace, Maria," my mom told me. "You'll have it forever. You earned it".

That is the time I started to think; No, I started knowing that material things didn't matter. Nothing mattered to me besides the real things I longed for and didn't get. Love. Compassion. Comfort ... and Peace.

At my party, the song *Wind Beneath My Wings* came on and I thought of mom right away. The song was fitting as she was always in the background taking the heat while she encouraged me to move on without her. If she only knew that all I wanted was to be with her and have the love and family I needed. Mom was such a special woman, absolutely everyone around her loved her.

FAMILY TRADITIONS

I would always look forward to Sunday Dinner upstairs at my grandparents. It was kind of my safe haven from it all. Grandma was strict, demanding and calculating. Everything was a routine and she could come across mean but was just focused and held us accountable for our actions.

Mom didn't cook all that much, so eating at Grandma's would be common for us. Well, she did cook, but wasn't all that creative, she definitely wouldn't make it on the show "Top Chef". And you could tell she didn't really like to cook. She didn't make the traditional Italian Sunday sauce or baked macaronis so much. (Even though macaroni is automatically plural, we have to add the "s" at the end, it's an Italian thing).

Though she wasn't traditional with her cooking, Mom would prepare food for us. We didn't starve that's for sure! Chicken cutlets were her specialty, pounded extra thin.

"Of course," the butcher replied. "Extra thin, of course."

She would make chicken cutlets on a Monday and then we would have left over chicken parm heroes the next day. She would then cut the cutlets up cacciatore style on Wednesday. Then, on Thursday, she would make something else and cut it up and pour gravy on it for the following few days. Fridays, once a month, would be liver with onions and ketchup, whether we liked it or not.

Like it, I did not. But, of course, I ate it up like a good domesticated little girl. It was about consistency and she was certainly consistent; a lesson

I am thankful for learning from her.

FEAST OF THE SEVEN FISHES

On Christmas Eve, we would have The Feast of the Seven Fishes. *Yes, we like to pluralize words unnecessarily, remember it's an Italian thing.*

We would start off the Eve with cold antipasti which was a platter of olives, supisad, provolone, capicola, spicy mortadella, roasted peppers and fresh mozzarella *(pronounced mootzidel)*. Then out would come the hot antipasto starting the first of the Fishes, about three pounds of breaded and fried shrimps made with 4 Seasons breadcrumbs and pure Italian olive oil. Next, we would make the fried or grilled calamaris *(pronounced galamad. Not sure how the gala or the mad came about, but that's how we pronounce it.)* The scungilli *(pronounced scungeels)*, and then the lobster meat.

We would make the bacalau, which is a salted cod fish. I would not eat the bacalau. I just couldn't get it down, I don't think anyone really liked it since it was not served in my house the other 364 days of the year, but as per our tradition it would be on the table. No matter what.

The sauce was always homemade. The razor thin garlic, oil, fresh pepper, salt and spices would simmer all together all day long, getting stirred only with the wooden spoon. You never use a metal spoon to stir the sauce since metal will remove the sweetness from the tomatoes, just like the domesticator did to me. He was my metal reaction when he stirred me up.

We would always have baked macaroni, such as lasagnas or baked zitis. None of my favorite meatballs would appear on Christmas Eve. Instead, we would have breaded and pan-fried chicken cutlets, and some kind of veggies, usually broccoli rabe. Italian bread, some wine and the salad at the end would complete the meal. Well, before the rainbow cookies and stuffed cannolis, *pronounced ganolis.*

I loved to eat. They used to joke with me when I would sing along to one of my favorite songs and ask "what did you do with the money your mother gave you for singing lessons" my quick reply was always, I ate with it.

Food mmm …

Every year, Christmas Eve would be all day eating for us and each and every year I would get sick. I know it doesn't sound like a far stretch to assume mixing or eating all that food would lead to getting sick. You wouldn't have to be a nutritionist to figure that out. Even when I would take my time or cut back a bit, I would still get violently ill and vomit everything up that night and the next day.

My sickness was bad and didn't make any sense to me. I would be doubled over in pain and going to the bathroom was a challenge. We didn't acknowledge allergies back then so no one brought up that I could possibly be allergic to something I was eating, so each year I would gorge at The Feast and get sicker and sicker.

It wasn't until years later that I realized I inherited diverticulitis from my Grandma. Diverticulitis is a condition where pouches form in your colon and can fill with bacteria and become infected. It is very painful. Ask anyone who suffers from diverticulitis if what we ate on Christmas Eve would make them feel sick.

They will say, yes.

All those years, I hadn't realized what I was doing by eating things that were making me sick. It was just tradition, what I was taught, and I never looked into it.

We need to be aware of the signs around us. Many people go through life totally oblivious about the situations they are living in that can make them sick.

SUNDAY DINNERS

Sunday Sauce was not only tradition but an institution that would require the prep to start the day before and the stove would be on from early morning before church. After church, we'd stop in town for a fresh loaf of Italian bread and then head back home to finish the sauce.

I would get to help Grandma with the sauce, open the cans of crushed tomatoes, a sprig of basiligo, chop the garlic super extra thin like in the mobster movies, and gather all the items to simmer together in the pot.

To me, it was the smell of "home".

Every part of Sunday Dinner came from a specialty store. Grandma's specialty was a dish called Spedini. I remember ordering the beef from the butcher on Long Island; they had the thinnest. It had to be cut super thin and long; Everything else would come from Ragtime or Brothers on the Boulevard. Sometimes we would drive to 65th Street in Brooklyn to pick up sausages. The mozzarella came from another store.

Back then, the only reason we shared dinner together each week was because it was tradition. So, it was mandatory, and you wouldn't want to know what the consequences would be if you were not there.

Every Sunday I prayed we would become a real loving Italian family but that didn't happen. We would sit around the table and pass the bragiole, the pasta with sauce, or gravy depending on who you asked. Then the chicken cutlets and the bread. We had what seemed to be a happy Italian family dinner.

But it was a fugazie picture of a happy family dinner.

It was an illusion. A fake, a facade, a fugazie.

NEW YEAR'S EVE

We would throw our annual New Year's Eve Open House and everyone would be there. We had music, family, friends, drinks, food and everyone would have a blast.

The domesticator would be smiling and happy. It felt good, for a little while ... until the next morning.

I couldn't believe how someone could act one way in front of his friends and when he was alone with his family, a switch went off and everything was "doom and gloom."

He was two faced. I never wanted to be like that. I promised myself in those moments that I would never wear a mask. I would be the same person ... consistently.

The way he would speak to Mom, to me and all of us was a part of who he was. His moodiness was unpredictable so walking on eggshells would be an understatement.

Saturday mornings I knew the call would come as the sun would rise and shine in the window. "Maria!"

Cleaning time for me. I dared not to hear the call more than once for fear that I would get it. "I'm coming".

"Okay, clean up time, we have to get this house in order," he demanded.

We, of course, meant me and Mom. The women in the house would clean while he would sit back and click his remote.

I would see the mop and the broom and the bleach and look around for my evil stepsisters like in the story, but only one evil person was to be found. The domesticator.

Mom would always be cleaning too. I'm not sure if she actually liked cleaning or was trying to help me out. Either way, I think that is why she didn't cook that much. Not cooking meant no messy pots and pans and not having to hear about it.

FIRE ISLAND

So, about the good times. Vacation!

I love to travel and back then I would travel with my family pretty often.

My entire family; my brothers, uncles, aunts and cousins would pack up and off we would go. I loved hanging out with everyone. The long days on the beach; evenings at the arcade and the family time was amazing to me.

In New York during the summers, we would spend almost every weekend on the water and take our boats over to Fire Island.

Fire Island is a part of Long Island that you have to get to by boat. Well, you could technically drive to the beach in the winter months, kinda like Daytona beach in Florida, but for most of the year it was walking or bike riding only.

There are dock slips on the bay side of the

island and the boardwalk has bars, restaurants, hotels and stores. Homes line the oceanfront. It has beautiful beaches with rolling waves as far as the eye could see. Beautiful blue skies in the day and fiery sunsets at night.

Getting there was half the fun.

All the women would go with the domesticator on his fishing boat. Meanwhile, the men would hop on the "Crispy Critter," *that was the name of my uncle's cigarette speed boat.* A cigarette boat is a power speed boat with top speeds of 86 knots or 100 miles per hour. My uncles, brothers and cousins would all hop on.

"Wait for me," I would yell, as I ran towards the boat. I always went with the men to get some time away from the domesticator who was driving the women on the fishing boat.

On the cigarette boat, the engines would roar with a loud *vrmm vrmmm* and physically vibrate even louder than the roaring engine. Mom would worry that the noise would deafen me. I loved the thrill of the ride! I was scared to my bones but wouldn't show it. I didn't want to go on the slow boat with him. I was the only girl on the loud speed boat and loved being part of the thrill. The ride was super fast, flying full throttle the entire time. The wind would whip my hat or sunglasses right off my head, but nothing could wipe the smile from my face.

It was a scary ride, yet nothing was scarier than being with the domesticator so I showed back up every single weekend, getting pushed around and teased as the little girl on the boat with "the men and the boys".

Every chance I got, I chose to ride the speed boat with the men. Even if it meant suffering through rough weather, pounding waves, with my butt banging down on the seat and my head down counting the minutes to land. It didn't matter. I was free.

The Crispy Critter would always get there first.

I learned how to tie up the boats and put everything away to keep safe. Then I would go and help the women when they arrived. I loved that even more. Getting there first meant I was prepared and could receive the women and help them off the boat.

We would dock on Ocean Beach and take over the hotel; rooms, the hot tub and the club. VIP style, of course. It was a glorious memory. I would always feel safe because my uncles would be around. They kept the domesticator in check. They wouldn't stand for any of his actions and at the same time they respected his privacy in his home.

No bad days would happen in front of family and friends. It was the highlight of my childhood. I was free on Fire Island and protected with my family watching over me. Nothing bad could happen there. It was my sanctuary.

To this day, Fire Island is still my sanctuary and I spend time there every summer. The early September sunsets are always my favorite. They are some of the most beautiful sunsets this planet has to offer. I love to walk on the beaches, write my stories, ask the universe impossible questions and quiet the noise for a while.

During those long summer days, I would walk the beaches and imagine my future self breaking free. I would have my sit down with the Universe and ask why. As I grew older, I learned not to ask "why?", but to ask better questions.

"Why" is just a word that keeps us circulating negative thoughts and we never really get an answer that serves us. It is better to ask who, what, when, and where questions, like:

"Who am I, who do I wish to become?"

"What can I do to improve?"

"Where is the lesson in this situation?"

As I walked on those beaches, I decided to just be. It is a perfect word, "Be". It doesn't even have to have an explanation. You know what it means to you by the feeling you get when you hear it. *How does it feel to just "be"?*

I knew that if I let it be that everything would be perfect. It would all become clear to me as I allowed my life to unfold and not fight against it.

I asked the tide to take my hurt and pain and turn it all into happiness, joy and love. I imagined all the good I did coming back to me with the returning tides.

The beach became my alchemist.

MY SISTER BY CHOICE

I worked from the age of four counting cars at our family's car lot keeping a log of all the colors, makes and models and how much they sold for. Over the holidays, we sold Christmas trees and I kept track of those as well. At the age of 15, I started working on my own. I worked at a family friend's bagel store making the egg sandwiches and cutting the cold cuts. Then I worked at my aunt's store selling shoes and clothes.

When I wasn't happy with what was showing up in my life, I chose to change the path to keep pointing back to where I wanted to go. Many would call this determination, I call it being relentless and "the only way I would have it". It is amazing to know that each and every day we have the opportunity to redirect what we don't like about our life and change our story for the better.

After high school, I had to make a huge decision. I was offered an opportunity to work at JFK for Airborne Express or I could go to college. The choice was mine.

I chose to sign up for college.

After graduation, I started at Kingsborough Community College. Six months was all I could do. Once I realized there wasn't any real money to be made playing cards in the cafeteria and nothing coming out of hanging on Manhattan Beach, I decided to go for the job at Airborne Express.

Because of my family, I had an "in" with the union heads, so I was pushed ahead of a lot of applicants and got the job.

To get into Airborne Express you had to type 60 words per minute. I probably typed about 25 words per minute; most of them misspelled. I was responsible for the data entry of over 100 air bills per hour and typing 25 words per minute, that wouldn't be possible. People vouched for me. To vouch for someone in my circle was a really big deal. They trusted me and I would not dare embarrass them.

So, I practiced and typed. I typed and practiced. I was task oriented. I wanted to be the very best and make them proud. You say I need to type sixty words and one day I will type seventy words a minute.

The night shift was the only one available to me, which was fine because it gave me freedom. I worked 11pm to 8am. If I wanted to hang out one night, I simply told the domesticator I had to work.

I fit right in with the team on the night shift. I felt safe and protected. I was feeling a new sense of freedom. Airborne was full of great people who looked out for their own and the crew became another family for me, after my blood relatives, block family, high school Stella sisters and my closest friends of course.

Leading up to my 21st birthday, I took all the overtime I could get to save for my first vacation without my parents. My whole Airborne crew was going to Cancun, Mexico. That is, until the domesticator chimed in and forbid it. *Really? I work full time. I'm an adult. I can't go away with my friends for a long weekend that I'm paying for all by myself?*

The trip wouldn't have cost me anything because of my perks with Airborne. It would be a sin not to use those perks. I just need to pack a bag, pay the taxes and get on the plane. This wasn't a dream I would let pass. All the dreams I let go of before were lessons on how I was not going to live.

This was the last time I would be controlled by him.

Or so I thought.

He told me, "Go and you can't come back in this house". This was the first time I understood I had to leave on my own. I'm not sure if I was more excited to get on the plane and vacation with my friends or that upon my return I would be free. Either way, I quickly packed my bags and never returned. I left without Mom and without my brothers.

Just me, myself and I.

I traveled all over with a great group of people and had an incredible time.

And the domesticator's threat really wasn't all that threatening. It was the words I had been waiting to hear.

It was a promise that I absolutely knew he would keep. You see, as bad of a person as he was, the domesticator ALWAYS kept his word. So off I went, knowing nothing for certain besides that everything in my life would change.

But how would it change?

I didn't know. I just knew, from that moment on … I was in control of my life.

It was scary to leave my family and be all

alone, but nothing would be as scary as staying in the cage I was brought up in forever.

From that moment on, I would be the creator of my life, and that was all that I really wanted. I had a choice and the pivotal moment was before me. My entire life was changing. A new paradigm. A new definition of me was unfolding. It was the moment I had waited for my entire life.

When my plane landed back at JFK, I moved in with my grandparents, upstairs from the domesticator. I took over their living room and slept on the pull-out couch.

Living with Grandma meant I wasn't under his rule any longer but I still had to see him almost every day. For more than a year, I wasn't really free.

I had to serve another year of time all the while planning my escape.

And then suddenly, the day came.

On my next birthday, my cousin and I got a

place together. She and I were cut from the same cloth. We both worked at JFK, and were searching for security and change. She would be closer to work and I would have a roommate.

My neighbor had a house he was looking to rent, and we took it for $500 a month. An entire house for me and my cuz!

I was working full time, hanging gangsta style. We were the coolest and toughest females to hang with. Everyone loved us and our company in the neighborhood. We were watched and protected all the time.

We were happy, safe and free. I was out from under the domesticator. I broke free from the abuse and the fear. I was safe and it was a perfect escape.

The funny thing was I was free but not free. I was physically free from him **but not mentally**. I still heard his voice in my head and the crack of his belt. *This would take some time.* I had it under control. I was in charge now.

And I would figure this all out.

After a few years, I started the morning shift and met a whole new team of co-workers. On the very first day I met a person I would refer to as my sister by choice for the rest of our lives. The night crew told me we were exactly alike, and boy, were they right. We formed a sisterly bond almost instantly.

She lived in Canarsie and we spent every moment together. We hit it off straight away; as if we knew each other forever and I was introduced to her crew. They had a hard time letting me in and my gangsta sista had to vouch for me. It wasn't too long before I was one of them. Part of their crew.

My sister and I would go out dancing every single weekend. Dancing like nobody was watching and music are two of my power sources to plug into for mental, physical and spiritual survival. During this time of my life we would go dancing at many clubs: Jams, Sprats, China Club and later on, The OZ. We always had a hook up with the bartenders.

$20 tips kept the booze flowing. It was great.

I introduced my sister to a guy friend of mine
and they hit it off right away and married soon after.

The wedding was filled with feathers,
diamonds, great music and some really big hair.
Fabulously, Howard Beach, head to toe. They came
up in a cloud of fog from under the dance floor.

She moved away from her friends and family
and slipped into her 'wife' label pretty quickly. I
missed her; we all did, but we were domesticated to
get married, be a good wife and the natural next step
would be to start a family.

And not to question anything.

A few short months after the wedding she
arrived on my doorstep with her jewelry, an overnight
bag, the clothes on her back and her car keys. Even
though we were all taught that divorce was not ok,

she was my gangsta sista. She walked away.

She moved in with me right away, and for the next few years we slept head to toe in the same bed. Yes, I said the same bed.

We were each other's support, comfort, security and life during those years. We did everything together and we were all we needed.

Over those beautiful and transitional years, she became my sister and her parents became my family too. Separately, we had nothing; but together we had everything. We both walked away from what other people would look at with envy.

My friends would tease us and probably thought we had more than just a platonic relationship. I didn't blame them, after all what two grown women really share a bed? There was a love growing between us and for the first time I felt what love would be like.

The seeds of love that were planted as a child by my Aunt were starting to take root. I always imagined what love felt like and now I was actually experiencing it.

We bonded and formed a love that would last a lifetime. We were sistas, not blood sisters but Gangsta Sistas.

Head to toe we stayed. We laughed, worked, danced and traveled together. Our friends and family judged our relationship. I felt my brothers didn't like her and gave her a hard time.

Why? Did they think she was taking advantage of me? Teasing me? Our friends, too, would question who was paying for what. All I could think was *wow, people have a lot to say about things they know nothing about.*

I helped her find her freedom and she provided me a priceless love I hadn't ever felt before.

She would be another angel in my life. But in those moments I started to become paranoid.

Paranoid of the ''what ifs''.

What if she leaves again? What would I do?

What if I don't find a family? Or someone to care for me?

SOUTH OAKS

I was starting to feel what love was, for the very first time, love without fear. My best friend was my roommate and life was great.

Then my paranoia came true. The floor beneath me collapsed from under my feet. My very first living angel, my beautiful Aunt Eva passed away from Breast Cancer.

It was so sudden and so severe to me. I knew she was sick, but to actually be gone? I mean gone gone? It was so final. The death of my idol, my beautiful angel who always doted over me. The most beautiful woman I had ever known, both inside and out. And now she was gone.

Who would continue to help me develop my new feelings and continue the excavation of this thing called love that was forming in my soul?

Her death hit me like a ton of bricks. Death hit me. Life hit me. The lost time, the hurt, the pain, the ultimate disappointment and lies of my childhood.

My heart pounded, the skin on my forehead beaded up with sweat. *It wasn't fair. The domesticator was spreading fear and she shared love, and now she was gone ... and he gets to stay?*

My face felt hot, my palms sweaty. I couldn't eat, sleep or function. My eyes swelled up and I couldn't hold it in. For the first time in my adult life water started pouring from my eyes and down my cheeks. I cried laughing before, but it was different to cry from missing and loving people as an adult. It was a funny feeling, the water from my eyes dripping down on my pillow; soaking it each night. *So weird.*

As a child, I used to cry, but was trained to hold back the tears and suppress my feelings. All of these "feelings" started breaking through the cracks in my wall.

What was this? A sign of weakness? A sign of inferiority? What was going on with me. Was I going soft?

One day, while grieving, I was drawn to my bedroom mirror. I didn't recognize myself. My eyes were red and swollen. I was panting and heaving from the emotion rushing up from my insides. As I held my head in my hands, tears running down from my eyes, I heard a great whoosh in my brain, like a balloon that was untied, and all the air rushed out.

Whoosh, POOFFFFFFF!!

A real noise that didn't have volume, but great depth rang in my ears and changed my vision and perception immediately and forever.

All the emotions I buried came rushing out of every pore in my body. It was like a rusted shut valve had opened and emotional energy was running full force, absolutely nothing could stop it, not even my domestication.

I could not stop crying. Day after day, I cried. I cried in the morning. I cried in the afternoon. I cried in the evening. I went to work and cried in the bathroom stalls. I went home and cried myself to sleep. I went outside and cried. I stayed home and cried.

I cried a lifetime of tears. I cried for myself. My mom. My empty bank account. I cried because I didn't know what love really was. I cried for my murdered dolls, my broken upbringing. I cried over the distance between my brothers and me. I cried for my entire life.

I knew I couldn't go on like this. How could I do this every day?

It wouldn't be possible. My fears were becoming reality.

One night I awoke in a panic. I started to get visions of my mom being murdered just houses away from where I was living, and that I wouldn't be able to help her. My mind started playing out my deepest fears and I thought it was real. I didn't know how to deal with these feelings and a great fear set into my being. I was crying all the time and having visions I couldn't share with anyone because they would send me to the looney bin. So I did what anyone else would do to help the situation … I decided to quiet it all and tune out completely.

I was no stranger to alcohol and drugs but I started to use more and more. I liked the feeling of taking something on Friday and Saturday to keep me mellow. I would take a valium and wash it down with a few beers and maybe smoke a joint. It would mellow me out when the noise got too loud, that's all. It helped drown out the noise inside my head. And it worked, the visions would become blurry.

I only use on the weekends. I'm not addicted or anything.

It worked. But only for a little while; until the weekends got longer; which they always do. And the voices got louder, which they always get. At this point in my life, I was living every day on weekend status just to get through that one day.

The noise was turning into actual voices and the nightmares were happening in the middle of the day. Life was fading from brightly covered up clouds to pure darkness.

What is happening to me? I'm so confused and so filled with fear.

How can I handle this without finding a large enough crack to end this forever?

The days and nights are tougher now. Things are going from kinda blurry to blurry all the time. The visions and the voices are the toughest to deal with, I cannot wait until my friends and I would go on that trip to Miami. *A vacation, that's just what I needed!*

My trip, when was it again? I think it's the day after tomorrow, that's so long away though. *Just a few more days Maria!* The panic sets in. The heart palpitations, the lump in my throat and the sweats.

Hello? Did you say something? Where are the voices coming from? *That's weird.* Not so bad though. Nothing I can't handle. The violent visions are the scary ones and they are starting to happen all the time.

They are just visions though, they aren't real. Right? Aren't they?

My heart is pounding, my hands sweat, and I am trembling. But nothing is happening.

Maria, calm down! *It's all in your head.*

The phone rings. *Mom, is that you? Are you safe? Are you hurt? Hello Ma? Are you there?*

No one is there.

Just one more day.

I am getting picked up tomorrow by my friends and then off to Miami for some much needed R&R. I just have to get there, it is my salvation. The mental stuff is bugging me out. *I am not equipped to deal with this!*

The visions keep coming.

My baby brother being tossed out on the street. Me on my own. Childhood memories flashing before my eyes. More visions. *They won't stop*!

My uncles going away to prison. My father and his brother not talking to each other.

My family was torn apart. Mom wasn't allowed to see her own bestie. He forbid her. The domesticator tore everyone apart.

My beautiful aunt going to be with God.

Visions of Mom's death.

Hurt to euphoria to grief. It was just way too scary. The loss of my childhood, insecurity about my future; *what would I become when I grew up and who would care for me? Who would become the family I had longed for and not ever leave me?*

All these feelings and my self medication was taking a real toll on me. My friends and family were all trying to help me, consoling me and assuring me that everything would be okay.

I just needed to get on that plane. South Beach. Just a day away.

"Keep your head up, Maria."

"Just push through it, Maria."

And of course, "This too shall pass."

All words to me. Compassion was something that, on top of all the hurt, was foreign to me. When I think of it, I was never consoled before. Not inside my home anyway. No one ever held me tight and told me everything would turn out good. Compassion was a new feeling. I was never spoken to with compassion and true love at the very same time. What a wonderful combination. What a wonderful word - compassion. A beautiful word but it was all way too little and so very late.

I'm that broken egg that everyone was trying to glue back together; but all the king's horses and all the king's men couldn't glue me back together again. I was broken, hurt, filled with fear of everything and very,

very sad.

Mom, why aren't you answering the phone. Are you okay? I'm so worried about you. *Was she okay, or did something happen to her? Was she dead? Should I go to the house and check on her?*

There is no one to answer these questions.

I cried, laid still and prayed to my angels for a sign. An answer. Something that would point to what was real. What could I believe? Who could I trust? How long would these feelings last before they would be taken away from me? I spent the night before my much needed escape to Miami crying my eyes out, shaking and filled with fear and blurriness.

What was real and what was not?

Someone packed for me. Or maybe I did? *I'm so grateful for good people in my life.*

I just needed to drown out the noise. I need my music again. Music was always there to soothe my hurt and transform my tears. This time the music was different. I turned on the radio and heard people talking about me and when the music would play, I heard the voices being directed to me. I started getting delusional and the self-medication wasn't working any more. I was lost in a fog.

A "dollamogue," as my future father figure would say. He would describe a dollamogue as a time or place of mental confusion or a time where someone would be lost in the fog. It meant cloudy thoughts and unfocused behavior to me. I was in a dollamogue. Searching for love and the feelings that I have longed for my entire life.

Was I delusional?

I had no answer. It was just me and my thoughts.

My male bestie from Canarsie picked me up with another friend that afternoon.

Beep! Beep!

He's here! I grabbed my things and ran to the car. We have to take that ride to Long Island. *One stop to help a friend and then off to JFK.*

I was getting anxious in the car. *Let's go, let's go!* I wanted to be sitting on the plane getting ready to take off, but I knew we had to help our friend first.

"Are we there yet?"

"Just a few more minutes now, Maria."

Finally, we arrived at the airport. *This was the longest drive I had taken anywhere.*

We pulled up and grabbed a spot, pushed through the swinging doors and arrived at security. The little trays appeared, and my pockets were emptied. Out came my wallet, keys, my smokes, glasses, pack of gum, my favorite snacks and a handful of change. My bag of clothes was next. *We were just going away for a long weekend trip why was there so much stuff? Oh well, off to South Beach!*

Security opened my bag to go through it, "Come on guy, what do you think I put in there?" *Seriously this is taking way too long!* They started to count my items and log them in a book. I turned to my family and noticed they didn't have any bags. *This was weird.*

Then I heard the words that sunk my stomach to the floor. "South Oaks Maria, we are at South Oaks Mental facility. We are not going to South Beach. We had to bring you here for help. We are leaving you here with these people who will help you".

I fell into the chair behind me. *What is happening?*

The steps keep getting foggier and everything is spinning, *didn't they say we were helping a friend? That wasn't me they were talking about? Was it? I was going to South Beach … um … in Miami … um … in Florida. It was planned, we planned it all together.*

I was watching my movie from the outside, thinking this was all happening to other people around me. I could even smell the popcorn. But it was happening to me.

I was sitting on the couch with my head in my

my hands. I remember feeling sorry for the person who was struggling and hearing voices and wishing to help them. I really wanted my friend to get the help she needed. *But was that me who needed the help?*

The staff started asking me questions. *Um, why are they asking me questions and all looking at me like that?* I started crying for my friends to take me with them. The staff let them know that it was all right. My friends wept, kissed and hugged me and with the sound of a swinging metal door, I was alone. All alone.

I am just fine. I just need a vacation. That's all.

South Beach… um in Miami. Thats all I need. There would be no voices, visions or confusion there.

Don't leave me here! I'm scared, I'm so scared.

I tried to explain to the hospital staff that I am okay and that there was a mistake.

"We'll take it from here," and the doors shut. I ran toward it calling out for my friends & family and was quickly restrained by the orderlies.

"Calm down. It will be okay." But calming down isn't that easy when you don't know what is happening and you watch your family's back's as they scurry out and you're alone. I'm a strong girl, angry and not wanting to be controlled or restrained. I did what I was good at - I defended myself. But I was no match for the professionals.

I felt the prick of the needle and fell lifeless into their care.

Today I can refer to it as a breakthrough and a break free. But back then, in that hospital bed, in the straitjacket with the stirrups and the needles to keep me out of it, it didn't feel like any kind of breakthrough.

I had a complete and utter mental breakdown, kinda like the movie Girl, Interrupted.

No, it was exactly like that movie …

… but it was all happening to me.

South Oaks Psychiatric Asylum is in Amityville, Long Island. It is one of the best facilities on Long Island for crisis management, treatment, and recovery. It was a trek for my family to visit me, but everyone came.

One by one, my brothers and their wives. My mom. Even all my newly ordained musketeers from Canarsie came. My Airborne Crew. My aunt came with my favorite stuffed artichokes. My cousins came.

Then the call came from the domesticator. My brothers told me he was on the Southern State Parkway on his way to come and visit me.

That's when my breakdown really started. I couldn't imagine the thoughts going through this man's head that would make him think it would be all right to come see me in my darkest and saddest time; all of which he was at the steering wheel for creating.

I started to cry uncontrollably. My brothers

told me to calm down and they would handle it. I don't know what exactly was said between them, but it would be the last time the domesticator would ever think of coming again.

Ironically enough, this institution I was forced to stay in would turn out to be the protective walls where he couldn't get to me. It became my safe place where I could not only think but start to feel as well.

Something inside me knew that I needed to be there. I didn't know why, but I would breathe through it and another moment would pass.

I had to face my demon, the domesticator. While he was not able to visit, he was still living in my mind and body. I realized he was there because I allowed him. The demon I was facing was one I was creating each day. It could only exist if I let it.

What if I can break free from the hurt and pain of the past? What if I could be free from the mental noise, sadness, confusion and the dollamogue? Can I really take charge of my life and navigate safely to peaceful thoughts and find true love in my life?

All of a sudden, I wasn't scared anymore. I knew if I was able to live in his home all those years under his constraints, a straitjacket wasn't gonna do me in. Each time the needle faded, and I awoke, I learned to let go and just be in the moment.

I knew I needed to break free so I could become a different person … so I decided that I could decide. That might sound crazy but crazy was all I had. *Can the peace and love I seek from others be hidden inside me?* The moment was finally here - being in charge of my life. It was all my movie. I was writing it all from inside the asylum.

I realized I was directing everything, including the insane asylum. Realizing that I wrote that part in, I now knew that I could write something different. I could also write the part where I turned my life around, right? *I think I can anyway and that is good enough right now.*

The days were long and the nights dark. I was

alone to face this head on. Realizing that I was all I have in life, I chose to start on a journey to find love. The love I didn't have as a child I was determined to create for myself. I decided in that moment to use this time to face my demons and come out victorious. I was in charge. I knew I could learn to turn down the volume on the noise and maybe one day remove it all together.

I chose to lower the volume and concentrate on me.

It was an interesting project and I had nothing besides time on my hands, so I took the challenge head on.

I focused and cleared my thoughts through a sifter and only kept the positive and supportive ones, the ones that I deserved to have in my life. When the negative or scary thoughts came to the surface, I would breathe through them in an effort to connect with my inner peace. My demons wouldn't be fought with violence but defeated by creating space for peace and tranquility.

How? That was the question that plagued me. How, with this "disorder" I was now labeled with, could I get myself better? Is it true that the tiny pills have the answer for all I've endured? *Could they change me and erase my pain and hurt? Could they help me become happy, start an amazing career I would love, help me help other people or even find a family and the love that I'm missing inside?*

Could all my bad thoughts be parts of the old movie? And could that movie's end credits be playing right now?

Could I really create a new movie? Where would I start? I would like to create one not based on hurt and abuse but based on moving forward. If the old movie wasn't able to be deleted, I needed to be okay with just storing it away.

In order to move forward I first needed to take a look back.

I started to ask the tough questions.

Who am I, and who do I want to become?

What do I really want to do with my life?

What is my life's purpose and am I willing to do the work to change?

I had faith that this was a positive life changing experience for me so I went with that option.

Everyone was praying for me. Each time somebody visited I could see the concern and sadness on their face. At the same time, I wasn't worried. I knew I was just visiting this place. *I am passing through here!*

After only a few days, my Baby bro wanted to rescue me; he wanted me to be "fixed" already. Even though I would be tied up in a straitjacket and was only allowed outside during certain hours of the day, I wasn't broken. I had my thoughts to create my life. Every moment mattered. Every thought mattered.

I didn't know which thoughts were real and which were fake yet. I prayed and decided that the fake ones would fade to black and the real ones would come into focus.

Each day the orderlies would come and give me medication to keep me "out of it" and each day I wouldn't take it, just like in the movies. Day after day, the same assembly line of little cups with the same little pills. Day after day, the same stick out your tongue to make sure I swallowed them. And then spitting the pills out right after they left.

I would sit by the swinging doors every morning waiting for them to open. I imagined all my friends, loved ones, family and neighbors on the other side of that door. They were all waiting for me to run through those doors and celebrate life. There were balloons, cake, and noisemakers. A celebration for me breaking free from the walls and chains that have defined me.

One morning, instead of imagining the walls of my room crushing in on me, I wanted to try something new.

Staring at the stark white walls of the asylum, I sat back and directed my new movie. I imagined how my life could be if it were up to me and played the 'what if' game. *What if I could start over? Not as an abused and unloved person, but as a strong woman. Could I direct the rest of my life?*

I imagined a great life where I could be proud of the woman I was. It was filled with love, so much love that it poured out of me. I rehearsed what my life would look like and told myself that when I am ready, I will press record.

I directed the movie in my head that everything would be changed. I imagined a life that was filled with joy. Real joy, not just the "happy go lucky joy" that was covering up the real hurt buried inside. The real happiness was there, just out of reach. But I saw it, more clearly now, just behind the doors.

Thinking back to the early years, many things are still blurry for me. I have had challenges visualizing. I did so much work early on to block the pictures and many of them have been deleted forever. I was happy enough burying my feelings because that meant they were gone, but I was finding out that's not the truth. The truth was they were still buried inside me and still very much a part of me.

I continued to bury my feelings until I hit this rock bottom with no more room to dig.

I woke up one day and heard Dionne Warwick on the radio talking to me.

I couldn't make out the song, but I knew it was her. She was talking to me! She couldn't get to where I was, but she wanted me to know I was safe. She told me everyone was having a party for me just behind the swinging doors and it was just like I had imagined.

She described the guests, the music, and all the wondrous details of the party. She told me all I had to do was walk through the doors and join the party when I was ready.

It sounded amazing but I couldn't do it. I wasn't ready yet.

I created a story in my mind that I was physically incapable of walking through the doors and leaving, even though I was sitting twelve feet away from them.

I was like an elephant that is chained from infancy and as an adult elephant a small string will keep him locked in his space forever.

I was in a bad way during those days but something inside me told me what I really knew to be the truth. What I have always known, no matter which prison I was in.

I was stronger than this.

I was stronger than the circumstances I found myself in.

I knew this situation was temporary and would pass. I wasn't meant to live the rest of my years as a volunteer vegetable, tied up in a bed with my ass hanging out the bottom of a hospital gown.

This too shall pass

I chose to refuse the drugs.

Every day. Every time. No exception. No excuse.

Although I felt broken, I was certain the tiny pills in the cup couldn't cure me. I knew that drugs only numbed the pain and it was time to deal with the pain head on. I was the only one who could help me. I found out that I did have somewhere to turn and that was within. I had my internal mentor to help guide me … it was Me. My own inner Mobster was becoming my own inner Mentor. Learning how to switch from one to another, in my opinion, is pretty gangsta.

Going from Mobster to Mentor was no easy transformation. In the darkness of night, I rehearsed the scenes of my life and held tight to the new visions. The old negative visions were strong, and we wrestled each and every night. I wanted to bet on the positive each time, but the old negative visions pinned me most nights. Then it hit me, I'm safe and always have been safe. I am now able to sit in the moment and simply be, even with the fear.

I decided not to run from all the ugliness, the darkness and the sadness.

Absolutely all of it. And yes, the fear. I was searching for the lesson, instead of asking why I was there. I was there to think and direct my new movie, I kept telling myself. It was all about me and my decisions that would literally create the rest of my movie, I mean my life.

I made it through another day!

I knew my war scars would help heal someone else's pain one day, so I knew I had to start with healing my own pain to prove there was a better way to live. *Once I prove my theory, I will share it with everyone in here. I'll help them all break free from their mental chains as well.*

I wanted to tell them that my mental breakdown did not define me and I would create the rest of my life ... and so could they.

I wanted to share the messages I would get in the night, but realized that no one would understand and then the orderlies would pay special attention to the pills piling up in my garbage. *No, I can't chance that. For now, it's just for me.*

Each day I wished to share these revelations with everyone in the place and let them know it doesn't have to define them either. *Not yet, Maria. Not yet. Soon.* Whatever prison we put ourselves in: mental, physical, emotional. All prisons are escapable. *I will escape them all, one by one, I just know it.*

It wasn't over for me, it was just a new beginning.

In order to have the love I craved I needed to learn to love myself first. I realized I didn't want to check out, not yet. I still needed to play this game and make conscious choices that would help me grow.

After the doors finally opened, I walked out a very different person than the one who was dragged in kicking and screaming. The feeling of freedom surrounded me once again. Freedom is scary though. I took a deep breath in through the nose and out through the mouth and pledged right then and there that I will not screw this second chance up.

I know there is work to do and just because I walked out of there doesn't mean I'm completely whole again. It just means that I chose to fight and face my challenges head on. No facility can help me long term, I must do "my time" on my own. Though they were unlocked, I still felt the chains around my wrists.

In South Oaks, I realized I wasn't happy with my life and that I could choose a different life where one day I could help people transform and shape their lives. I started thinking differently than what others had taught me and started searching for something so much grander. *Where to begin changing my life now that I'm on the outside?*

I am spending most of my days at work and I hate my job.

I was taught to work at a job I didn't love for forty to fifty years and then retire with a gold watch and a handshake. I was tired of running on the hamster wheel. I wanted to help people. I wanted to let them know that what they were experiencing was all a story created by them.

And stories can be rewritten.

I knew I couldn't just talk about the changes I wished to share with the others, I had to be the change. The changes I needed existed inside of me. I had to change. There was no chance I would ever be able to star in the movie I was writing by trucking along the same old way I had been taught.

I couldn't use the mobster, angry way I learned from the domesticator and I chose not to use the lying ways I learned from Mom. I chose the path of love and faith and with that decision every thought would be transformed from anger to love and from disappointment to faith.

"DEAR D ..."

A short while back, during one of my dark, dark days, my childhood friend came to visit me. She brought a special gift just for me, a new diary. I thought it was such a nice idea but writing for me was about as foreign a concept as learning a new language. I wasn't ready to find out what was behind that door.

Now that I'm officially out of South Oaks, I keep the journal or diary, or whatever you call it, next to me on my night stand and look at it every day. The pen is in my hand and my eyes squint shut but no words come out. My lips stay shut and no feelings flow through my body into my pen and onto any of the pages. I just can't imagine it at this time.

Maybe one day, but not today.

With my lips shut tightly, I picked up the pen again but wouldn't allow my feelings to flow onto the paper. *What can I do, maybe I just have nothing to say?* It's silly, I thought. But deep down inside I didn't think it was silly, just a foreign language that I wished to learn.

Each day I would wonder, is today "one day"? I just can't imagine it at this time. *Soon, very soon.*

One day, one of my Canarsie friends came by and picked up my pen.

She began to write:

"Maria, I know things are hard and maybe not even making sense right now, but, in time, there will be no more darkness and no more unsureness in your life. And with time your scars will just make you stronger. Not better, because you are already the best. If I haven't ever told you, I will tell you now, you have not only been the greatest friend, but one of the signs of strength in my life. Thank you for being so special - C".

And there it was, as plain as day. I had to decide.

I was special and others needed me to be stronger, better and free.

To simply… be.

My story is special and my hurt will heal, my unsureness will become a pillar of sturdiness for myself and for others to lean on. It had to come out, it had to be told and it had to be written. The pen would become the code that would unlock my Omertà.

The credits rolled on my new movie. I grabbed my pen and wrote the first words that came to me.

"In the beginning …"

What should I call you? "D" for Diary came to me …

"Sometimes I feel (really think, not feel - I haven't mastered what feelings are yet) like I'm the only one that could ever understand what I am going through. So why not write to myself, or God, or the Universe or to you, D.

All I know is I'm starting to have what my doc said are feelings and emotions for the people I love. It's scary. Very, very, scary. Since my breakdown, my emotions have become absolutely unmanageable and I am just learning how to 'deal' with them.

I feel like I am being misunderstood by absolutely everyone, that I am a burden or I'm giving too much of myself. I fear I will ruin the beautiful relationships I have. Maybe I should back down, but that isn't the way I want to be. I am struggling whether I should share - even with you, D.

Sharing my true feelings is scary. Will my 'love' feelings push my friends away?

I am where I am today D, because of not sharing love. Maybe one day I would understand this new world that I'm starting to explore, then I could get these emotions under control and perhaps even master this feeling thing.

Before my breakdown, I was happy go lucky and had that 'do what you gotta do' attitude as sort of a mask. This is the only way I knew; cover up and don't share anything.

Who knew what it felt like to miss, care, worry, cry, be sad, depressed, lonely or even have compassion? Or have a realization of other people's feelings? It is just so new to me and I am trying so hard to keep everything under control.

I told myself that I was going to separate my thoughts and feelings and gain some control of what was actually happening.

Where did this come from? Oh boy, where do I start?

"This goes deep, very deep, D. My drastic change is becoming noticeable to others, even those who didn't know about my breakdown. I have to get away from everything familiar to me and reprogram my mind."

Moving out of the house I was renting with my cousin in Howard Beach was the biggest decision I made after coming home. I needed to retreat, but also needed safety and protection. My sister and her family lived on Staten Island, so I wouldn't be alone and that felt safe.

"Yes D, I said Staten Island. I know, I know. But I rented a nice apartment by myself and will have time to work on me. It's just going to be for a short period of time, I'm thinking like six months. Just enough time to clear my head. My Gangsta Sista is going through a divorce and it is bringing up old memories, thoughts and feelings that I used to have when I lived with the domesticator.

Wow, this is scary. I was made to be a

protector, designed to help others learn to walk away from unhealthy situations. I want to help people change their lives and I am broken and can't help my own sister or even myself right now.

For now D, I will work on me, sorry, we will work on me. Together, yes together. Night Night".

I thought this would be the story of the rest of my life, so the next day I started writing again. I wrote and wrote and wrote what seemed to be my entire life over the course of the following few months. The second I felt the pen hit the paper, I knew this would be a tool to help me break free.

"Dear D. Okay. I'll talk ... so I need to talk to you about what happened before I checked into South Oaks. Weeks before, some scary things started happening to me. One night, I couldn't get out of the car to go into the diner after the club. I was showing up to work at Airborne and spending time in the bathroom crying uncontrollably. I couldn't stop the tears day after day.

I am still not sure if I am losing my mind or if I'm gaining a new mind. Sometimes I think I might be making more of my problems. Maybe I should have stayed in the straight jacket a little longer? I feel it would have been easier to knock the tiny pills back and check out for good. It's so frustrating!"

Missing someone, caring for someone, worrying about someone. Who would have guessed this was me? This was all new to me and so confusing. I never felt anything for my family except fear. I never explored any of the love feelings for them or anything real.

What was the word love all about? I did love them. I think. Then again, I didn't feel or even know what love was. I would do anything for my people, like a mother cheetah fiercely protective of her cubs. *Is that love?*

Love is a new word for me. I enjoy learning new words and new ways of speaking. *Okay, to hell with it, let's explore what it means. What have I got to lose? I already lost my mind ...*

I did really lose my mind already and it ain't so bad. I am climbing out of the dollamogue.

"Hey D - So, my psychiatrist from the asylum insists I continue seeing someone now that I'm on Staten Island. Not healthy to leave everyone and everything and move to another borough without an outlet to keep exploring."

That led me to the day when I met Dr. Larry.

"I had a very stressful week, D. I need a drink, but first I will make my appointment to talk some of this out. I have no one really to talk with besides you and not for nothing, I'm looking forward to getting some feedback, no offense."

Dr. Larry told me whenever I feel empty and nauseous it is because I'm scared and fear the unknown. He said that emptiness is a place of fear.

"What do you fear?" he asked.

I told him I want to go to massage school and fear I'll never be able to go. I mean, where would I get the money from anyway? Do I quit my job that my family vouched for me in? How will I support this silly dream? I also fear losing the relationships I've made.

"I have not spoken to my mother in at least FIVE days, D. She called me today and I really had nothing to say to her. She is a stranger to me at this time. I have no feelings for her. I can't share what I'm going through with my family or friends. I can only tell all my thoughts and feelings to you. In a strange way, when I write to you, I'm getting some answers. Go figure?"

"Hey D! Tonight, I went to Dr. Larry and we had a very good session. I told him about my breakdown/breakthrough in some more detail and we really got deeper than last time ... well as deep as I am willing to go with him at this point.

We spoke about my emotional addiction toward my new crew and why it's so deep. Dr. Larry told me I'm very strong and my story is very interesting. He still can't believe I was in and out of South Oaks without taking meds so quickly. He never heard of that before. He called me an anomaly. Remind me to look up what that word means.

He didn't understand how I went from being in a straitjacket to helping other people inside the institution in just six days. Getting someone who didn't take a shower in what seemed to be weeks, to care for herself and bring a smile to another person who hasn't cracked the sides of her cheeks in months? And my great sadness is that I couldn't take them all with me. Oh right … it's about me first and then I will help others out of the darkness.

We spoke about those dark nights, the new things called tears, my fear, anger, disappointment, depression and mourning the loss of my childhood. This digging is so draining … Dr. Larry says I have to do the work and that wonderful things will happen." *I knew this was true, I would beat this whole mental thing. … But it's lonely, I can't lie.*

"Dear D, I am very scared today. I hate coming home to no one, nothing, just emptiness. A cold and lonely space on Staten Island. I feel empty. I'm not sure what's worse, dealing with my fear and anger or dealing with this new thing called loneliness. How do I express my sadness? I can't. I was never allowed. How do I start now?

I'm definitely in search of a loving family, I want and need it so badly. I will attract this to me, D! This beautiful family. I'll have love, fulfillment and won't be lonely ever again. Then my life will be complete." *It's just on the other side of the door, Maria, just on the other side, remember that!*

"Oh God, how do I stop feeling so down? It's not me. It's not who I am or who I will become. Why do I feel like just giving up sometimes? I could check back into the institution and be another number in the system like my doctor was talking about. It's probably easier than this stuff." ...

... "Time goes by so slowly now. I guess I'm hard on myself because this is what I was domesticated to do. I learned everything was my fault and the world required and needed me to 'fix it all'. I was Wonder Woman, able to do, fix and solve everything. Even things I couldn't understand. Reality sucks! No one understands me and maybe never will." ...

… "It's only me. I haven't heard from my family in some time. Family is so important to me; how could I not have one anymore? Do they care about me? Do they know how to care about me? Maybe they can't communicate because of their domestication too? Part of me knows they love me tremendously. Dr Larry keeps assuring me that they do. It's really scary to feel let down all the time. I'm really alone. All alone." …

… "Life is a big struggle and for the past four months I have been really, really alone. I knew the Staten Island thing would be rehab for me. No noise. A quiet place I could go and think and still be near my gangsta sister and her family, but I never expected this deep loneliness. Not even when I was locked up in my room to think about what I did wrong as a child.

My only goal is to have a happy, healthy life and a beautiful family. But it's hard …" *It's just behind the door Maria, the hard part is over. Focus, Maria.*

"Dear D - I saw the domesticator tonight and he was mean. It is so insane to watch everyone accept him and all his rules as if he's some sort of 'Don'. I mean the guy is a wanna be - no real man treats and controls his family like he does and then expects them to kiss his ring. I don't want anything to do with him." ...

... "I'm crying, again, D. I have never cried like this before. I thought the crying was over.

This is not like the other type of crying though - it is different. Something new. I can't really explain it. Dr. Larry said it is new and healthy to get out some old "feelings". Even though the domesticator isn't in my life, he controls everyone around me, and I think that's part of why I feel so sad and lonely. He ripped out parts of me I will never get back, the best parts - my love and my family." ...

… "Guess what D? I am done with Staten Island. I'm moving back to Howard Beach. The last five months was a great escape. It was the dark night of my soul, my meeting with the darkness life had to offer and I am officially done with it. I conquered that part of my life and met with every emotion that exists.

I learned the most amazing things about myself over the last five months. I used to feel that time alone was a punishment because of all the years the domesticator would send me to my room to think about "what I had done wrong". Now, I know it's a gift. It's like opening a gift wrapped in sandpaper.

It's time to move on from my exile.

I will miss Dr. Larry but I gotta go and start my path of happiness and joy." …

… "I finally got that party. D! All my friends were so happy I moved back to Howard Beach."

I moved into this two bedroom apartment in old Howard Beach right outside Charles Park. My gangsta sister moved back into my room and one of my Canarsie besties and her boyfriend moved into the second bedroom.

One day shortly after I moved in, I was awakened by the smell of meatballs. *Sniff Sniff* … and sauce and … mmm garlic. *Follow that scent*, I heard ever so quietly inside my head. In a weird way, that wonderful, all too familiar scent not only whispered for me to follow it but it told me that everything was going to work out. It told me that I was on the right path. *Oh my!* I had to find out where it was coming from. *Sniff Sniff* … This beautiful smell was coming through my vents.

Was this another illusion? A sign? Whatever it was, I was listening to the voice.

I grabbed my robe and crept down the stairs to where the smell of my grandma's cooking was wafting out from under the door.

Knock, knock. "Hello?"

Peeking in the door, I saw the giant pot on the stove. I walked in and saw a guy sitting on the couch. He looked up at me and said hello…

"I have to take a meatball." I walked to the pot, took out a fork from my pocket, and stabbed it into a fried meatball. "Mmm. Delish. Thanks, I'll be back next Sunday. See ya."

With that I walked out and went back upstairs.

As I mosied up the stairs, chomping on my meatball, I heard him laughing. "Moo, who is our neighbor from upstairs?"

His wife answered, "Her, oh, I don't know her. I never saw her before. I thought you invited her in?"

"D, I like reading and positive things now. I have been reading lots of helpful books. I read the best book ever. The Way to a Peaceful Warrior. It's a book that changes lives, well it's definitely changing mine. It has so much meaning and truth inside those pages. I used to have the tools for being tough and growing up in the gangster life; intimidating others came natural to me. Now I'm learning some new tools like peace and meditation and kindness for others. It's kind of cool and the best thing is I can still be my gangsta self." ...

... "I am trying to deal with emotions. I never learned a healthy way to deal with them, no rules or guidelines besides to instill fear, build your wall, don't let anyone in and don't bitch about it.' ...

... "Dear D, I'm very depressed tonight. The only way for me to survive is to build my wall back up. I always had one but it was broken. A crack was driven through it by me talking and letting stuff out. I tried letting someone in but then got hurt.

Dr. Larry would say that everyone is entitled to their choices and I don't want to get sick. I must keep breaking the wall down, but I'm scared. I'm trying to get in touch with my feelings on my own without therapy, but can I do it? I will have to strengthen my mind at least until I could see another doctor again."

... "Therapy, or the lack of, has been a situation for me since I moved back. Sometimes, I simply can't afford going over the bridge due to the out of pocket expenses. Also, I know I can't afford NOT to do it. I can't afford to slip back to where I was, D.

I can't ask for a referral closer to me from my family, because they don't know any local psychiatrists and if they did, we just don't talk about it. I need to talk to someone about what is happening in my life. I will look for someone closer. I want to continue. I must find another therapist."

It's a funny thing when you talk to the people in my neighborhood who had to do real time away.

The longer they're in there the more difficult it is to acclimate to life on the outside. There is no plan you just do your best.

The other thing is that when they come out of jail, they are respected and praised but I'm ashamed of the time I did and the hiding. I am definitely not going backward. Not going back there again. *I have to figure this out.*

"Hey D, I got myself in some trouble. I went out for a few drinks and some dancing. There was a dark-skinned guy I was dancing with who got me a drink and we went to the parking lot to chat and make out.

And poof … nothingness.

I can't remember anything besides the car, the leather smell, the sweat and the emptiness when he walked away.

I was slipped a mickey or roofie. My friend said I was raped but seriously, I was just taken advantage of, right? Even when I get drunk, I know what I want and don't want. I should have been stronger. Where was my superwoman cape?

I felt so yucky, the kind of yuck that I'm not sure I could talk or write about now. For now, I will try and forget it happened and protect myself better. Speaking of protection, I hope he at least used something." *Oh my God, what a nightmare!*

Now as I look down at my purple pinky nail, I realize I was part of the #metoo movement that would take another two decades to come to light.

"I was late this month with my period, D. I absolutely cannot believe this. Just when I was getting better, I am taking a step back. Last Monday I took the home pregnancy test and it came out positive. Now I'm pregnant from God knows who. Could I even raise a child when I still feel like I'm building my own self back up? Could I afford to take care of another person - I'm not even on my feet. I don't have gas money. I hardly have a car and have all the bills I racked up. And where do I start looking for the father? In the back of Jams' parking lot? It's way too much for me right now.

I am not ready for this." …

… "Tuesday, I went and did what I had to do. My gangsta sister was my inner strength through the whole experience. We went from love to death and to every single extreme in this lifetime. It was a very emotional experience for me but we made it through together.

God forgive me please!

I can't believe I was pregnant. There are no words right now …

So, I pray.

Today I have no words, Today it's just blank. Tomorrow maybe some words.

I will rise from this."

The next day at work, I grabbed the phone book and thumbed through each page of names and as my finger grazed the section of about page 350 or so, there it was 'Psychiatrists, Psychologists and Therapists". Then subcategories, Queens, and the list got smaller and then Howard Beach … and then the name, Snowman.

Researching him, writing down his number, picking up the phone and calling all felt like I was violating some secret code or doing something wrong. But I was just reaching out for help. I knew that no one in my circle would ever hang out with people named Snowman, so I was safe.

Consider it done. He is the man.

The Snowman.

THE SNOWMAN

I decided I needed to talk to someone even more than ever before. I held everything in for so long. All of my feelings, emotions and my tears until the floodgates opened and they all poured out.

I started to see Dr. Snowman. He was an amazing mentor and helped me see how our thoughts shape our lives.

Snowman taught me that it is not what we go through in life, it is how we process what we go through that shapes the rest of our lives.

I told him I wanted to find a life coach to help me propel forward, someone with a fast forward button and a plan.

I felt stuck and even though he was helpful, I needed something different. I am not afraid of change, I will do what I have to do.

When I told him I wanted to help others because of my time in South Oaks, he gave me some of the best advice I have ever heard.

"Maria, you have a gift. This very special gift to see beyond sight, to know without knowing and to have faith and belief in yourself to change almost miraculously ... that is just not normal. It is something extraordinary and now you must be careful, since you cannot save everyone. Not everyone is ready to cut through like you did and choose to face what you are facing without needing to medicate.

You will be a mentor for others, in time, but now it is your time. Work on yourself. Decide what you want to do in life, and find that life coach you're talking about. You're on the right path."

"Thanks, Dr. Snowman. You're a great help. I

know I am on the right path."

"Keep on exploring your gifts, Maria."

I smiled. "You mean how I came from such a dark place to such a better place now?"

He nodded. "Now that you have a special gift of seeing, you need to be very responsible."

I did just that. I kept the faith and little by little, day by day, my life transformed. I loved sharing, learning, talking and experiencing life.

I wonder if life coaches are listed in the Yellow Pages?

THE CONFRONTATION

"Dear D,

So, talk about being thrown a curve ball ... You know how I want to mentor someone and help them break free from their circumstances? Be careful what you ask for, as they say."

My 94-year old grandmother was complaining about having difficulty breathing and was taken to the hospital while I was away for the weekend at Cape May. They ran tests and discovered her blood pressure was dangerously high. She also began to babble incoherently. The doctors called me and told me she suffered a severe panic attack that was probably triggered from her PTSD. They also told me that they gave her some medication to calm her down and lower her vitals, which were "off the charts," but they saw no change in her condition.

"What do you need to do?" I asked.

"We will induce a coma state to allow her body to heal and intubate her to make it easier for her to breathe."

"You want to stick a tube down her throat?" *Okay. Tubes down the throat to help her breathe? Okay Doc, you know how to handle this… I hope.*

After a few days, there was no change to her condition and a hospital priest came to administer Gram's last rites. Seeing her hooked up to the machines, I'd do anything in my power to get her back. I massaged her legs with essential oils to keep her circulation going and massaged her scalp to keep her brain stimulated.

I spoke with her everyday even though the doctors and nurses told me she couldn't hear me.

"Hang in there Gram, don't let those tubes get in your way. This is just temporary. It's just a dream.

Soon you will be free from all of this."

I would share Reiki energy healing with her from her bedside and again when I arrived at home. I imagined with every breath she took she was growing stronger and stronger.

"Please Gram," I whispered. "Don't give up now. You will find that freedom you have always prayed for. It's just on the other side of the tubes."

I felt a gentle squeeze on my hand.

Almost a week later, grandma had a full recovery. The doctors removed her from the tubes and pronounced her perfectly healthy. I knew I couldn't let her go back to that house with him. It wasn't good for her mental or physical well-being.

I shared with her that I had a plan so she could live the rest of her life without fear and I would coach and assist every step of the way.

Even though she had always wished she could leave, she was still driven by her fear and prior conditioning. She would beg me not to intervene.

"I don't have enough money to afford to leave Maria," she protested.

"He'll never allow me to move out Maria, I just can't go," she complained.

"It's too late for me. I'm too old," she objected.

I knew she wanted a fresh start and to be safe, but I also recognized she was scared. I sat down with her and reminded her of her inner strength. I asked her to remember the times she was strong for me and my brothers and all the times she was strong for her daughter-in-law.

I knew there was a better life for her. "Please just trust me, Gram".

I solutionized the plan pretty quickly.

First I dealt with the money. I contacted the Veterans Association and found out she was entitled to both of her late husband's pensions. That, along with the little savings she had, would keep her living in freedom at an assisted living facility.

Next, I started to solutionize the plan of getting all her belongings. *How could I get all of her furniture and belongings when they were at his house?* I needed to get her things without the domesticator knowing. The plan was to get a U-haul truck and bring two people to help move her stuff while he wasn't there.

Gram asked that I take the grandfather clock. She cherished this tall brown, wooden clock with its shiny metal pendulum and she told me she wanted to pass it down to me. So that was the plan. The clock first then the rest of her furniture.

It was just me and the two helpers. We carefully wrapped up the clock and the two men carried it down the stairs, put it into the truck and drove safely to my house.

After a week passed we went back for the rest of her stuff. Bed, dresser, clothes, phone. Anything she would need. I couldn't miss anything because I knew I could not return after he found out everything was gone.

Coming back to this house where I was abused filled me with anxiety. My fear of having to confront him again was draining my energy. I couldn't wait until it was over and I felt safe again.

I was standing on a step stool in her bedroom when I heard one of the helpers coming back up the stairs and heard the floor board creek behind me. The hair on the back of my neck stood up. I was about to turn around when I heard the voice I feared the most. "What are you doing in my home?"

I turned and there was the domesticator. Seeing him made me nearly fall off my stool but I held in my inner trembles. I would not back down. *You will not intimidate me.*

I was face to face with him. Looking straight into his eyes. I expected to see that same anger and rage that shook me to my core. Instead all I could see was weakness, insecurity and confusion.

"Where is it," he screamed.

"Where is what?"

"My clock!"

"She gave me that clock," I said. "She always wanted me to have it and she told me to take it. So, I moved it out. It's mine."

In his rage, he demanded "his" clock back. Otherwise there would be no move. No belongings would make it past him that day or any day moving forward. She would not be let out of her prison.

Everything came to a screeching halt. He proclaimed that nothing was to move, including my grandma, until *his* clock was returned.

Now what? My plan was kiboshed and I needed a quick back up plan. The first thing that came to mind was to set up a sit down for her freedom. The clock for Grandma.

At the sit down the domesticator said, "Clock for the old lady … and she can't come back. She's cut off."

And I agreed.

So, the clock made it back to him and grandma won her new found freedom. In those late years of life she had another chance to write the pages of her new unwritten story.

I remember her thanking me and telling me that she is so happy. She told me what I did for her was unbelievable and I would go on to help many other people because I care so much.

Really, you just can't make this stuff up.

WORKING THE PLAN

Thinking back to my days in South Oaks, I wanted to save all the patients. I remember talking to them and pleading them to wean off the drugs and have a chance to 'snap out of it'.

Looking into their eyes, I realized then, even if I wheeled them out one by one that their own minds were their prisons, not the institution. Until thoughts change, there is no chance for us to change.

I would do everything in my power to keep my mind clear and work on what is important. I would care and give love to myself. I am on this journey by myself, but others are invited to join me.

It was the beginning of my desire to create my

path in life and choose self-love first. Once I figured that out, everything would fall into place.

It just takes one thought to change "why me?" to … "wow it's me!"

I'm ready for someone who can help me make decisions and hold me accountable for success and someone with a plan that works so I can cut and paste it into my life. I have goals to reach. The only thing that makes sense to me would be a coach. I played softball until college and wouldn't have made it without great coaches. They held me accountable for my actions, not allowing me to slack off. They pushed me to do better when they saw more in me than I did myself.

I was referred to this coach to help me reach my dream I now realized was becoming a licensed massage therapist. It was not so popular in the 90s but I had a feeling this massage thing would allow me to help other people heal with my touch.

The first thing the coach asked me to do was create a list.

"I love lists! I am the queen of lists."

"Good," my coach replied. "Because this list is special. This list will be the blueprint for the rest of your life."

The rest of my life. "Excuse me? I'm good at making to do lists but a life list?" I started to feel anxious again. I didn't know what my life was going to look like tomorrow. Snowman taught me to live in the moment and take it one day at a time. Now I need to write a list for the rest of my life?!

"Yes. Maria, if you don't have a plan for your life then you are planning to fail."

"I don't fail!"

"Then make your list."

"That's a big list. I don't know where to start."

"You start by making the list. Then you work towards crossing off each and every item."

"In order?"

My coach laughed. "Maria, the order you cross them off is not important. Only that you cross them off."

"What if I change my mind or life throws me another curveball or …"

He cut me off. "The list is simply a guide. It's not set in stone. It will change as you grow. And yes, life will throw you many curveballs. It already has. Remember, the order is not important. Crossing the items off is."

I went home and thought about what I really wanted in life. I thought about how I wanted to grow and who I wanted to serve.

I grabbed my pen and began my list:

    1. Dream job - Become a massage therapist

    2. Find Love & Family

    3. Lose Weight & Stop Smoking

4. Build a space where I can be a part of something great

5. Have an amazing life of travel

6. Know what it's like to feel safety, security and love. Lots of love.

GOING ALL IN

1. My Dream Job

"Dear D,

For a long time, I haven't been happy at my job. I mean it is okay, but It is not fulfilling to me at all. I knew when I walked out of South Oaks that I would find a new path in life. I finally know what I want to do. I pray to become a licensed massage therapist. I need to work with people, on people, to touch and heal people. I need to be touched by something real.

My coach thinks I should go for it and sign up for massage therapy school. For now, since I don't have any money for school, I'll buy a massage book."

… "Hey D, I read the book cover to cover and spent all my time working on friends and family to practice. My coach thinks this is great. Taking the steps is so important, however small they are. Some days I feel like a joke with my book and practicing. I may never be able to afford school. Is this real? Can it really happen for me? My coach thinks yes, and so do I!"

Every time I would focus on my financial obligations and object to my coaches' strategies, he would say nothing can stop you from your passion and your destiny. Stop focusing on the negative.

"But how," I asked. "How can I, Doc … I mean coach? It costs over $7,500 for school and with only the clothes on my back and more month at the end of my money, I could not afford it."

"Just visualize, Maria. Set your intention."

So I set my intention and took action, just like my coach said. *I'm putting it out there.* I soon had an interview at the Swedish Institute of Massage Therapy.

The day of the interview arrived. I sat down and waited for my name, worried if they would even accept me. *Visualize to actualize, visualize to actualize …*

"Maria? Is Maria here"

Visualize to actualize, visualize to actualize … Wait, what?

"I am Maria. Present, I mean, I am here." *Yes, ready. Ooh, my hands are sweaty. What if… shut up, Maria. Quiet. You got this.*

The phrase, "fake it until you make it" was at the front of my mind as I walked in to the office, looked across the desk at the person in charge and said, "of course I can pay this off." The truth was that I didn't have a clue on how I would be able to get the text book for the course but yes, I would pay it back.

They let me into school on a payment plan. *Seriously? Was this really happening?*

I had to sell all my jewelry for transportation. *I didn't need the jewelry he gave me.* But how was I going to pay for the tuition, books and a massage table? *It may take me 20 years, but I would pay off this loan. Hope my coach has a plan to help me pull this off!*

The universe stepped in again when one of my Canarsie besties bought me a massage table and some others picked up the tab for my books. I was going to school part time and working full time on opposite ends of the city, but boy was I doing it! *Watch me win. Yes, I'm winning.*

I was doing it … getting through school, commuting, working. Then the day came … decision time. I couldn't bear my job any longer. I had to double down and finish school, so I left my job at Airborne and went all in, full time.

I became a full-time student at the Swedish Institute in Manhattan and spent the rest of my semesters all in. I would have just enough money from selling my jewelry, the tiny savings I had and the few private clients I had been working on just to get me to the last day of school.

I learned about the muscles and the body and the skeleton, met some incredible people and honed my gifts and talents.

It was finally here. The State Boards! All the months of classes and studying like crazy, I couldn't believe the day had finally arrived. I was pumped to actually become licensed. It was just a day away and then life threw me a curveball.

My grandfather passed away on the day of my exam. I couldn't focus or even imagine taking the State Board. I had everything riding on this one day. I had no more job, no money and sold all my jewelry to get travel expenses to and from school.

The day of the test I was a wreck. I took a valium to relax and tried to focus. I arrived at the test center and saw a line of students stretching around the block. I looked at the metal door to the center and my mind whispered, "just behind the door, Maria". *Everything I worked for over the last 24 months was on the other side of those doors.*

The day of the results …

I couldn't focus and failed my exam. I failed the exam by one point.

I have no words.

"Dammit D - I failed my state board test by one point! 74 to pass and I got a 73. A 73! I failed. Maria is not a failure, it's not on my vision board and not on my gratitude list. I had it all on the line and now I fail! It just can't be. What will I do? There is absolutely no plan B. What can I do? I fight for what I want."

One effen point stands between me and my passion, my career and helping people. One point stands between the old me and the new me. One point stands in between my feelings of faith and the negative feelings of the past. I have been studying for this for so long. I have to get this point.

I couldn't afford the bus or hotel fare to go to

Albany where I had to go to fight for my point. Everyone said how challenging, actually impossible, it would be to win. And still nothing could talk me out of it. Even though they said it was useless, I needed my point.

"I am going upstate to fight for my point", one of my fellow graduates whispered. My ears grew about ten sizes. "Can I go with you?"

It was several weeks since I returned from Albany and met with the State Board. I stated my case in the best way I could. They asked me a lot of questions to test my knowledge. I'm still waiting for my response from my appeal for the one point. The only thing they said is that I should know by mid-July.

MID JULY, OK!

And then mid-July finally came … There it was … the envelope from New York State in the mail. Tearing into it would change my entire life. My heart pounded and my muscles tightened as I ripped it

160

open.

There it was, my point. I got my point.

Holy shit, I did it!

I was free! I am now a licensed massage therapist. All is well and it will only get better from here! I now know that my theory works! I wonder if it can work for the rest of my list?

I'll find out in time …

TRUE LOVE

<u>6. Know what it's like to feel safety, security and love. Lots of love.</u>

I am looking to meet someone special. I confided in my friend from work about my desire for love. She really seems to understand me. I knew she was bisexual and I was curious about the whole thing.

Then there it was, my first experience: It just happened.

"Dear D, I had an experience with a woman. I wanted to tell my gangsta sister, but had a problem finding the right time and place.

Friday night we went to the club. I bought the

first drink and I told her. She was floored and then got upset. She felt lied to. She called me a lesbo. By the end of the night I think I argued her down to a label of bisexual. It didn't matter what she called me; the hurt was still there. I still consider it only an experience. Couldn't it be okay to explore without being labeled?"

Months went by and I felt once again that no one really understood me. It took me some time but the more I explored this side of who I am, the more comfortable I got with it myself and the more I realized that, yes, this is who I am.

I am gay. Shortly after that experience I decided that I'm coming out - out and proud!

Well, not so proud. More shy and insecure to be honest. There's no shame in my game, it was just a little weird. It was different. I was different. Everyone will get used to the new me now that I was getting used to myself. I knew my sister would come around. And she did.

After all it's still just me.

I met my boss the day I graduated from the
Swedish Institute. She hired me to work in her spa.
For two years, we worked side by side building the
business. Sharing the highs and lows. We would hang
out after work and dance and drink.

One weekend my boss and I were at the club
they filmed Saturday Night Fever in. I was supposed
to hook up with some chick I met on MySpace. We
never connected. I really wanted to make out with
someone and was complaining about being stood up.

My boss turned to me. "I'll kiss you."

"Hey D,

All is very well. I'm falling more in love every
day since the last time I wrote. Actually, me and my
boss fall more in love every time I write you and
every time we talk and … just all the time. We share

a beautiful relationship and I'm so very happy."

The years rolled by. We rented an apartment in Pennsylvania, spent long weekends together. I would learn true love from her and her gracious family. They aren't relentless like me about tasks but the one thing they are relentless about is love and I'm so glad to be a part of that!

"Hey D,

Guess What? I asked her to be my life long partner and she said Yes!"

We purchased a two family home on Staten Island. The idea was to live on one floor and rent the other out to cover the mortgage payment. A big magnolia tree with beautiful pink flowers stood in the front yard. The house sat on a quiet corner in a suburban neighborhood. *Suburbia, me ... this is what I wanted. Not trains running all night and planes flying overhead. This was perfect.*

"I can't wait to move in." I grabbed my life partner's hand.

"Not so fast. We need to cleanse it and design the interior with Feng Shui."

"Fung what?"

She laughed. "Feng Shui. It's a practice of moving furniture and choosing colors to create positive energy."

"Oh, cool." My life partner is a Feng Shui practitioner and she wanted to create the perfect loving environment for us.

The best thing about our house? It was only eight minutes from our business that was growing up. A couple of more years and a few more chess moves, we purchased a building and expanded our business from a couple of rooms to a three-floor luxury Wellness Center.

"Hey D,

The Green Spa and Wellness Center!

WOW, such a story to tell. It is now a wellness center. All grown up and three stories tall! OMG totally outrageous. We pulled it off through all the struggles. Men at work, contractors, sleepless nights, architect plans and so much testosterone … It was finally ours and a beautiful masterpiece. The first and only Green Spa in New York … probably anywhere.

We were pioneers for change and awareness and it feels amazing to be a trailblazer in this organic, eco, earth-loving, non-toxic, vegan world." I still wish to mentor and coach someone in a meaningful way.

GREEN SPA

<u>4. Build a space where I can be a part of
something great.</u>

We built an amazing business over the years,
allowing us to help countless people get through
physical, mental and emotional pain. We combine
physical therapeutic touch therapy, energy healing
with emotional support, hypnosis and coaching
programs to help people transform their lives.

Together, with my life partner and her sister we
have grown tremendously over the years. Three
women were able to successfully purchase, gut,

renovate, and build the first eco-friendly luxury spa in Brooklyn, New York.

But it wasn't easy. We wanted to use recycled denim insulation in the walls. Every contractor told us it couldn't be done. It was too expensive. That we didn't know what we were talking about because we were women.

We had to purchase all of the eco insulation in New York, New Jersey and all along the East Coast from Maryland to Boston.

Everything was taking longer than anticipated. It was frustrating, but then I remembered that empires aren't built in one day.

We were building an empire, not just something for the short term.

So, I kept my eye on the ball and relentlessly made the moves that helped one day lead into the next. Until the day my partner's cousin came to our rescue. He brought a team of people and took control of the job.

It was done right and quickly from that moment on!

Hyper focusing on my growth as an entrepreneur with our newly expanded company required me to enhance my communication skills. In order for our business to keep growing I needed to learn new skills. Networking, public speaking and communication. These skills would be imperative for my company to grow.

One of my clients told me about this group of people who met for breakfast every Wednesday at 7a.m.

"Did you say 7 a.m.?"

"Yes," he smiled. "And some come at 6:45 to set up. Trust me, you won't regret it."

The next Wednesday I showed up at 6:45 to see what it was all about.

There were about 25 business professionals, all specializing in different fields, from different areas,

170

sitting around tables, eating breakfast and talking about themselves. They shared what they did and what a good referral would be for them.

During the meeting the president shared the group's core beliefs. I heard the words loyalty, structure, team and rules. I was in. This was going to be the trusted group of people I would work with to help strengthen our businesses.

A team of business owners who vowed to support each other through referrals. *Yup, this was for me.*

Every meeting began with the introduction of the members and guests. I watched and listened as one by one each person stood and gave their 60 second commercial. Some were eloquent, others weren't. *Boy, they got their stuff down.*

Then it was my turn to stand. I realized a few things:

1. How overwhelmingly shy I felt. My face

grew hot, my palms were sweaty, and my voice cracked.

2. I needed a spiel. I think for the very first time I realized the importance of being able to quickly and clearly explain who I am and how I serve others. People judge people, and within a minute or less they decide whether or not they like you or would use your services.

3. This was much different from a sit down. This was a stand up. A *"stand and project my voice, refine my speech and communicate precisely what I was looking for"* up. It was a real challenge for me to speak and ask aloud for what I wanted.

My determination to do better, become better and improve led me to hire a business coach. We went to work on what would become my presentation. I wrote it out, said it out loud and threw it away. And started over.

Again and again.

I did the work. It's all I know how to do.

I practiced and practiced and couldn't help the feeling I got inside my stomach when speaking in front of people. I realized I didn't know how to present myself to the business community. I would be representing my company. I needed to break everything down.

My coach had me answer a bunch of questions.

Who I am? What is my title?

What do I do? Who do I service?

What would be a good referral for me and why?

I needed an educational piece or a catch phrase so they would remember me.

These questions made me break down who I was and how I wanted to be known.

It was, and still is, an incredible experience and took me from being super shy, fidgety and awkward to being very comfortable talking in front of people.

Being on top, having the best reputation and a kick ass business put us in the spotlight. Everyone wanted to work with us. After studying our market and looking into our next steps, we chose to expand with an existing hair business on Staten Island.

The owners of the shop approached me and my partners at the spa to help them expand their property and bring our proprietary services and concept to their space.

Their space was old and needed updating but had potential.

We put up all of our savings to renovate their building. We designed the space, paid for a website to be built, trained the staff and started implementing structure where there was none.

But we made a crucial mistake. We didn't protect ourselves. We didn't have a signed agreement. They stole our identities, money and what felt like our souls.

We found ourselves losing clients, $88,000 in debt, and not having enough money to meet the upcoming payroll.

The problems we were having in the business started taking its toll on all of us. I was fighting with my partners. All the negativity was tearing us apart and we were spinning out of control. I was about to lose my business and the love I fought so hard to find.

Then an amazing thing happened. I was introduced to a new coach at my local BNI meeting.

She was a life coach and was passionate about helping people. She shared stories of being down and out and how she turned her life around.

I knew she was the one to help me repair my relationships with my business partners and family.

For six months, I focused on repairing my thinking. I took responsibility for everything that happened.

Orly gave me new tools and taught me a new language that helped me let go of the hurt and shame of being scammed. She led me to a time and a place where I could deal with the enormous debt that hung over my head.

Then we looked for someone who could help us get our business back on track the same way Orly helped us with our relationships. It was a risky decision. We were hiring someone we couldn't afford to help coach us out of massive debt we couldn't pay. It didn't make any sense, but I had faith.

The business coach had us implement several small changes to build a team atmosphere. Even though I thought them to be silly, I was willing to try.

The name badges, daily huddles, and partner accountability sessions all worked and we were able to pay off the debt in less than a year and save our family business.

In addition to the coach we hired to help put our team back together, we needed to clear the bad energy from the spa. We called in our Feng Shui master and twenty other energy masters.

One by one, the masters entered the space packing an arsenal of uplifting energy weapons. They arrived with their intention cards, energy clearing smudge sticks, red envelopes and bells - just to name a few.

The air was thick with the familiar smell of incense and sage burning as I entered the large open space on the third floor of the spa. This was the starting place for our Feng Shui and Space Clearing Ceremony.

The South wall of the room held a beautiful mosaic of Buddha made from recycled glass. In the center of the room stood a hand carved Tibetan wood table that served as the altar. A homemade tablecloth of red and gold draped the altar. The imperfection in its stitches making it perfect.

In the center of the altar stood an illuminated rose quartz that bathed us like the sun gently lights up the morning sky. Around the rose quartz were candles, crystals, red envelopes, bells, feathered smudging wands with crystals on the handles and sage. A green jade Buddha and a white marble statue of Kuan Yin flanked the table. Blessed rice, colored red with cinnabar, sat off to the left in a crystal bowl. *Can rice be blessed?*

The blessed rice was passed around for each of us to sprinkle in the red envelopes where we would place our intentions for this space, our lives and everything in between.

I'm sitting and meditating over my intentions for my space, my life and this one day. The seats that are set in a circle around the altar are starting to fill up, everyone in deep thought as to what powerful thing to write down and place inside the envelopes.

A fresh and pleasant aroma filled my nostrils. *Mmmm.* Sniff. *What is that? Citrus? Sniff. It's orange.* I opened my eyes to watch our Feng Shui Master, RD enter the space. He is carrying an ornate bowl of the carefully selected oranges that we will peel and use to cleanse our space. *How are we going to use oranges to spiritually cleanse this space?* Before I could whisper my question to my neighbor, someone starts by throwing the peels around the floor. *Oh, I get it, we're not using the oranges, but the peels.*

We start to chant. "OM MA NE PAD ME HUM ..." Starting softly and steadily growing in volume until the vibration danced on our skin. Nine times we repeated the sacred words followed by the ringing of the bells.

It's time.

With the aroma of fresh oranges hanging in the air, RD told us to stand. A pungent smell, like unwashed underarms, assaulted me. One of the healers was standing in front of me with a sage stick burning in a shell. She fanned the smoke over me with her hand, cleansing me.

Each one of the healers moved to a different room in the spa. They took their gongs, bells, smudge sticks and began to cleanse our space.

I entered the Couple's Room ringing my bells. I stepped over orange peels that were dotting the floor. Healers stood in each corner holding up bottles and spraying the walls with Florida water. "What the heck is Florida water," I asked.

"Florida water is a blessed water made of alcohol and essential oils. It's like Holy water."

Holy water, I knew. My family poured it into small fonts which hung on the inside of the main door of the house.

In another room I heard the sounds of Tibetan singing bowls. These bowls don't actually sing, they sound like an angel's voice when you glide a mallet around the outer rim of the bowl, like when my gram would check the crystal stemware by rubbing her finger around it to make sure it wasn't a fougazie.

In room after room, chimes are ringing, drums were banging and people were chanting to cleanse the whole building. An orchestrated racket of sound to heal. Mini gongs and Tibetan bells getting louder and louder. Our Reiki Master floats in and out of each room. Her hands bright red from the intensity and fierce clapping. *Clap, clap clap clap clap.*

Each and every brick received their energetic butt kicking.

After the cleansing we all met in the basement. My ears were ringing, and I could feel my body vibrate. I looked around me and knew the others were experiencing the same.

Atop a table sat a small Tibetan Spirit House. There are no doors on this house, only little steps leading into it and carved openings on all sides. Inside we placed an offering to the spirits, a cup filled with alcohol. It was like spilling a little for my homies. *Pretty cool. Respect.*

SPIRITUAL AWAKENINGS

5. Have an amazing life of travel.

Spending all these years with my life partner, I learned about spirituality and energy. I wanted to connect with nature and my inner spirit in a meaningful way to fill in some of the blanks.

We were thinking about where to go on vacation. I was all in for Vegas baby but my life partner wanted to go to Arizona and do some soul searching.

Arizona is a long way from New York City but she kept telling me it was precisely what I needed. I reached out to some friends to see who would like to join us on our getaway.

Everyone was in.

Arizona is really hot! The sun was shining down from what felt like heaven on our bodies as we lay by the pool in search of some refuge from the pounding heat.

Each day we would schedule a massage or a body treatment at the spa. Afterwards, we could take a walk, sign up for a yoga or vegan cooking class. Or talk with the American Indian elders.

Each night we were encouraged to let go of our electronic devices and unplug. There were no televisions, phones, internet service or any way to connect with the outside world.

One night one of the Elders encouraged the group to search for the reason we were really there; to search for the miracle we wished to find. He told us we would find it then and there. The group looked at each other. "I thought we were here to relax."

The Elder looked right at me. "Are you here for a miracle?"

I didn't know how to answer that question. *Maybe? If it's possible.*

The night after, while enjoying some piping hot coconut and toasted almond infused tea, underneath the moonlight with the millions of stars all around us, we declared our miracle and our wishes to the universe. We wrote them down, communicated them aloud, and offered them up to the brilliant stars - as the Elder had told us to do.

He told us that over the next 48 hours we would be taken on a great adventure and all of our wishes would come true. He said we were not to think about where we were going but to allow the adventure to come to us. The one rule to follow was not to follow any rules.

"How would we get on this amazing adventure without planning?" I asked.

"No planning. No thinking. Too many westerners are in their head all the time. They don't smile. They're just thinking, and they are not in their bodies. Be in your body and turn off the noise in your head. The answers will come to you from Nature. Now go and do what you are drawn to do."

With that, we all agreed. No rules, no planning and no thinking.

The next morning, I rose to the sounds of the amazing creatures of the canyon and watched as the sun began to creep up over the mountains behind us. When there was enough light to see, we made our way up through the canyon. An eagle circled above us as he did each morning. The birds and the animals all around the area embraced the day with their praise. They too, were connected with this great ritual.

We started our hike up the canyon. What would we find? We didn't know. We simply walked over the red clay mountain and breathed in the fresh mountain air as we hiked all the way up to the top.

We kicked up more and more rock dust that fell onto our pants and sneakers, turning them the color of salmon.

As we climbed each red rock and continued to ascend, we didn't talk, we didn't think, we didn't plan. We were in the moment. *This is what it feels like to "be".*

"Take a deep breath," one of us said, as we

turned into the last leg of the climb. "Look out there!"

"It is so beautiful and endless. The mountains seem to go on forever!"

As I looked out over the mountains, my mind drifted to my partner's father. *Terminal? What does that word even mean? They have to be wrong. We couldn't have only three months left with her father.* It couldn't be real. There has to be more we can do for him. She believed he would get cured and live longer than three months.

We left every bit of our energy on that mountain. Physically and mentally exhausted, each of us took another breath and another step until we reached the top.

I was in search of forgiveness. I wanted to let go of the hurt and pain and tear down some of the walls I built up. I had to visit some things I buried in order to move on with my life.

A funny thing happens when you bury things

in an improper way, they show up again and again. The rain, weather and circumstances bring them to the surface. I was angry, disappointed and very sad. I didn't understand that I had to make peace with this in order to be free from it. I needed to make peace with all the hurt and disappointment.

All of the abuse from men and women throughout my entire life were fading to black with each step I took.

What could it all mean? Could I get past this and transform? Could I actually forgive? How would that even be possible?

Another step, another breath, and another moment passed.

"Just one more!" I shouted from up ahead.

One by one we all reached the top. We were finally there, this beautiful place where the heavens seemed to reach right down and touch our shoulders.

The Vortex.

I have never felt energy like this!

It felt fresh, permeating and dizzying all at the same time. It was a place I hadn't been to before yet felt comfortably familiar.

We took a few steps to look around, in awe of this magnificent creation we got to experience; even for just this moment in time. And what a moment it was, a breathtaking moment for certain.

The energy filled up my emptiness, helped me carve a smile back onto my face and I breathed deep into my soul for the first time in a long time. It felt good to be back on top. One word came from my mouth. Forgiveness! What a powerful word. I forgive myself … and I forgive everyone!

And there she was, a strange woman who was barefoot and bejeweled from head to toe in yoga jewelry and crystals, dressed in aerial shrouds, and glowing as she danced atop the Vortex.

She didn't seem to be from this planet, she was filled with love and light. The words danced off her tongue with an ethereal voice, "Come here my earth child," she held her hand out to my soon to be sister in law. "I am LaRaSol, your Earth Mother from another place and time and I am here to share with you a message of great love from this beautiful universe."

We were all invited to dance around together. LaRaSol told stories about being our spirit mother and was sent to invite us on a magical journey beginning at 11 a.m.

"People have traveled from all around this planet to take part in this special journey and you're right on time."

We were in awe of what was happening and made the journey back down to the meeting place just on time.

There is only a certain type of person who would speak with such a voice and make such a proclamation to a perfect stranger. It was LaRaSol.

As strange and unbelievable as the message was, we decided to have faith that everything was happening just the way it was supposed to be happening. *No inhibitions, no judgements and no thinking. Just being in the moment.*

I was a human doing and not a human being. I would attempt to force things to happen instead of having faith they would work out. All the energy I put into controlling things in my life kept me from being free.

I didn't need all the negative people, places and things in my life. My life was absolutely perfect just the way it was. I was perfect just the way I was.

All the self-judgment and negative self-talk was left there on that mountain. *This was what the great Elder was talking about.*

When we reached the bottom of the mountain, we were just in time to take part in this auspicious Awakening Ritual.

It was 11-11-11 at 11 a.m. *Wow! Um OK, an Awakening ritual. I am feeling this.*

Goosebumps tickled each of us as LaRaSol

told us about the plan for the day. We were about to be part of something absolutely life altering.

We were led through the mountains just outside Sedona where the red rocks lined up all around us. We passed many cars alongside the road with license plates from all over the United States.

Our front windshield was filled with red dust when we pulled into a vacant spot next to a VW Bus. We got out and walked down a dusty path. A large number of people were gathered in a huge expansive circle. They greeted us as long lost best friends.

In the center was LaRaSol. She introduced us to Shaman Indians, elders, spiritual leaders and enlightened individuals from all over the world.

We all held hands, chanted, sang together and wrote special wishes on pieces of paper to be buried. It was here I buried old hurts and wounds with love and respect and zero doubt or hurt.

Three hours passed and with each moment the bright sun melted deep pain, hurt, negative self talk and limiting beliefs. All self doubt was erased. I loved this spiritual experience and also realized that I didn't have to go all the way to Sedona to continue to love and forgive.

I get it now! I'm in and not ever going back to fear. I am awake now.

BREAKING HABITS

3. Lose Weight & Stop Smoking

I'm not comfortable in my own skin. Each time I was going to a bar, party or gathering the thought popped in my head followed by questions.

"Will I fit by the chairs when I pass behind people? What if my belly rubs against someone when I'm squeezing through the space?"

My face flushed hot and wore my shame and embarrassment without uttering a word.

Now that we were getting the Green Spa healthy, I knew I had to get me healthy. My life experiences made me mentally and emotionally healthier. Now, it was time to work on my physical health.

I knew I needed to lose weight and I needed to stop smoking. I needed to transform my body and build a slimmer and healthier one. I was sick and tired of being sick and tired and dragged down by unnecessary addictions.

I looked for help in the same old places. Counting points, weighing myself every week, going off and on fad diets; followed by gorging on Oreo cookies and milk, potato chips and Roll N Roaster binges.

It was like riding the Cyclone at Coney Island, going up and down, filled with fear and hoping the ride would soon be over. The yo-yoing led to more pain. Something had to give …

Everyone's a gangsta until it's time to make gangsta moves. I needed to step up into my inner gangsta and make a serious change. I couldn't do it alone. I had been on this roller coaster one too many times and the ride was getting me sick.

I decided to reach out to a mentor to help me get rid of my addiction once and for all. It was a six month program that combined mind work along with acupuncture/auricular therapy to combat physical cravings.

SIX MONTHS! Why so long! Can't I just read something or go to a seminar or learn how to do this in a day or so? Then it dawned on me. No, I can't; because it was about creating new habits to replace my old ones. I knew I needed the guidance from someone who had done it already. Someone who ran this race and already won. *A six month commitment to change the rest of my life is a very small investment to have guaranteed success.*

My Six Month Journey

The first session of the six month journey was a group session. It was a 'mind over matter' type of seminar for the entire group that taught us about triggers. *Triggers… the only triggers I ever heard of was the trigger on a gun.*

I soon learned a trigger is something that we experience - a smell, touch, or feeling - which brings about a response. It may be a happy response like how the smell of fig cookies baking in the oven reminds you of holidays at Grandma's house; or a negative response like watching a sad movie reminds you of a past lover and you start to cry.

At the end of the seminar, we were given the choice of leaving with the knowledge we gained or digging in and really becoming a master. Most of the group bailed. I was gangsta.

It was all or nothing. I locked and loaded and looked back at the old life choices that led me to that day and leapt with faith into the new practices I was learning.

Over the next six months, I learned the science of saying, "No thank you" to what was not serving me. I learned I had a choice every time. I was not a victim. *Holy shit! It's the same thing Snowman taught me!*

Instead of walking away from physical and mental abuse of the past, I was walking away from my self-inflicted pain. I was reminded about visualization and how to create my ideal body image. The image of the person I chose to be. My inner mentor taught me to recognize my strengths and use them to overcome any challenges I would face.

I was in my power. The best part was I didn't have cravings. I didn't feel as if I was missing out. The more I cut out of my diet, the better I felt. I stopped eating anything white. No carbs, no flower, no pasta, ice cream, cookies, cake and nothing starchy.

I lost 40 pounds in just six months. And went on to lose another 25 pounds after the program was done.

And I have kept it off for over a decade!

Cigarettes was the next thing I needed to quit. *You got this, Maria. Just use the same tools …*

But quitting smoking was a bitch. I found myself sitting at the bars on the weekend and telling myself I'll start on Monday with every drag I took. Monday was the beginning of the work week and I needed something to have with my morning coffee to wake my ass up. Tuesday, I would crumple the pack up and throw it in the garbage in disgust that I was not in control, but every Wednesday I was rummaging for that pack. Thursday, I swore not to buy a new pack but bummed off strangers. Friday was the weekend and after a long week I deserved some enjoyment.

It's a game. Only one you can't win. *I'm only gaming myself. It is a lie.*

The cigarettes and the deep inhales are only so good for a second and then the judgement, guilt and shame is just too much. I'm sobbing like a baby. I'm so disappointed with myself. *Why can't I cut off from this like I did with the weight?*

The old tools weren't working. I needed to create some gangsta tools on my own. I sat down and thought about everything I learned from my mentors and thought about why they didn't work all the time. It just needed to be simplified. I focused on keeping it simple so I could use the tools anytime. In the end, I created my own 12 steps to success. Thinking back now, I cannot really recall the last drag I took, only that it was the last one I would ever take. Good riddance forever.

DREAMS DO COME TRUE

<u>2. Find Love & Family</u>

In early summer of 2015, we heard the announcement President Obama made. Gay marriage was now legal. It seemed the entire gay community on Fire Island were all gathered to hear the announcement. Cheers and celebrations broke out all over the island. I knew that was the moment to tie the knot with my fiancé.

We started planning our special day the next morning.

The overcast skies of the morning had left leaving us with a clear blue that stretched to the heavens. *Who would've thought that stealing a meatball all those years ago would lead to the perfect wedding spot?* We stood on the third floor balcony of our best friend's house and looked out over the beach. It disappeared into crystal waters. Around a simple white wedding arch sat our friends and family.

We wanted a simple foot in sand ceremony.

My goumadas were all dressed in matching cream gowns ready to walk down the aisle. The music started and they took the first step towards the guests.

Wait! It's the wrong song!

I had to grab my girls and find the DJ and tell him he screwed up! *I was not walking down the aisle to Here Comes the Bride!*

After a few moments, the sounds of a ukulele filled the air and Somewhere Over the Rainbow washed over the wedding. *Good.* I watched as each one of my goumadas got to the top of the stairs and then disappeared down the sand dune.

I got to the top of the steps. *My God, I can't believe this is actually happening.* I stopped to take in the whole scene. I wanted not to forget a moment. *Wait, who are all these people?*

Our simple ceremony with friends and family

had grown as everyone on the beach had set up their chairs and chaise lounges to watch me get married. *Over 200 people were crashing my wedding!*

I met The Boss at the top of the stairs, and he walked me down the aisle. I turned to watch my soon to be wife's Rainbow Girls. Each one held flowers representing the colors of the rainbow. Finally, she appeared at the top of the stairs with her mother and sister. She was beautiful in her flowing white gown. A picture of her late father was attached to the stem of her bridal bouquet.

RD stood before us and conducted the ceremony.

Each of us held a vase full of sand which we poured into a larger vessel that represented our bond and joining together.

We held hands and communicated our love and commitment to each other in front of our friends and family. I wished my cousins, aunts, uncles and the rest of my family were there, then remembered they all were there in spirit wishing us a lifetime of happiness.

I looked out onto the crowd and flashes of my long summer days on Fire Island dreaming about true love had become my reality. The claps and whistles were not just for us though. They were for love itself.

For winning, for coming out, for non-judgement, change and acceptance. The crowd cheered for living out loud, for bravery, for gratitude, for strength, loyalty and family.

They clapped for it all.

We rang bells, poured sand, lit sparklers, drank champagne, danced into the starry night and did everything we could to absorb every moment.

The moon was the largest I had ever seen that night, the only thing that could compare is the one from the "Honeymooners" old time television show. It was seriously huge and took up the entire sky. We stared up at it as we held each other on the beach and it was as if the entire world shifted from under my feet in the sand that evening and I was finally rooted.

I belonged. I was loved and I was complete.

After all I went through in my life, I found out that love really does win in the end if you have faith and make the choices to let love in.

Truly #lovewins every time.

Now that's Gangsta!

SEVERAL YEARS LATER ...

"So D ...

Wow what a journey we've been on together. It's so funny how time changes a person. I have learned that with time, dedication, patience, belief in yourself and access to the proper tools anyone can change.

Thank you D for being there for me through the good, the bad and the ugly. You have been by my side through the scariest and toughest times. When I was locked up in the looney bin. And you were there for the best ... when I met my wife.

You have been my safe haven. The place I turned to express everything I couldn't share with the world. You allowed me to explore and find my best friend and my mentor; me!

Together D, we stomped out the part of me that tried to keep me scared and controlled by the Domesticator.

We did it, D … well really, I did it. I now know that you were a part of me all along. Because of the work I did with you, I wrote my new story. One filled with love and strength and friendships. You helped me break my Omertà and learn to share my vulnerability, successes and failures with the world.

I am grateful for you D. You helped me form my new belief system. One that has allowed me to create my own simple 12 step program that works and my very own Mentoring & Life Coaching business. I am finally where I always wanted to be. My #7. A Mindset Mastery Coach & Mentor.

My story is not over, D. Until next time …

Stay Gangsta!"

THANK YOU!

Thank you for allowing me to share my journey with you. People asked me why I would choose to share the darkest, most intense and vulnerable times in my life with strangers.

I share my story with you to shine a light on mental health awareness and to break the silence of domestic violence. In order for the message to be heard, it had to be real and raw. I was blessed and lucky on my journey to have others support me, hold my hand, offer me shelter, words of wisdom, show me love and guide me in the right direction. My mission is to pay it forward.

I believe that we're not strangers. We are part of one community that just hasn't met face to face yet. We all share a bond in the pursuit of breaking free from something that has held us back.

Additionally, I truly want to mentor and coach people through the amazing process of breaking free so they may live their best life. It's who I am at my core and it's in my DNA.

During all of my days of journaling and digging into my life's goals, I didn't know it was all leading me to live out my fullest potential, destiny and greatest dream. That dream unfolded for me as a mindset mastery coach and mentor, supporting others who are ready to break free. Whatever that looks like to them.

Our coaching company, Transformational Gangstas, LLC, was founded to make that dream a reality. The toolbox we offer is filled with an arsenal of programs in place for those who are ready for lasting change and real solutions. Solutions to help get unstuck, find new practices, behaviors, language, patterns, and ways of thinking.

If you resonated with any of my story, let's keep this journey going. Join us over in our Facebook page and say hello. (www.facebook.com/ TransformationalGangstas) and visit our website at www.TransformationalGangstas.com

See you on the outside!